EUGENIO MONTALE
NEW POEMS

ALSO BY EUGENIO MONTALE

Selected Poems
Xenia, G. Singh, trans.*

*Black Sparrow Press

EUGENIO MONTALE

(NEW POEMS)

A selection from *Satura*
and *Diario del '71 e del '72*

TRANSLATED AND INTRODUCED BY
G. SINGH,
WITH AN ESSAY ON *XENIA* BY F. R. LEAVIS

A NEW DIRECTIONS BOOK

ACKNOWLEDGMENTS
The poems in this selection were chosen from Eugenio Montale's Italian books *Satura* (1971) and *Diario del '71 e del '72*, both published by Arnoldo Mondadori Editore. Earlier versions of the *Xenia* sequences were first published in 1970 in a Black Sparrow Press–New Directions limited edition. Some other of these translations first appeared in the magazines *Agenda* and *Mediterranean Review*.

F. R. Leavis's essay on *Xenia* first appeared in *The Listener* (London), December 16, 1971.

Manufactured in the United States of America
First published clothbound and as New Directions Paperbook 410 in 1976

Library of Congress Cataloging in Publication Data

Montale, Eugenio, 1896–
    New poems: a selection from Satura and Diario
del '71 e del '72.

    (A New Directions Book)
    Bibliography: p. 115
    Includes index.
    1. Montale, Eugenio, 1896–   Diario del '71
e del '72. English. Selections. 1976.
PQ4829.0565A28   1976   851'.9'12   75–31600
ISBN 0–8112–0598–3
ISBN 0–8112–0599–1 pbk.

New Directions Books are published for James Laughlin
by New Directions Publishing Corporation,
333 Sixth Avenue, New York 10014

CONTENTS

PREFACE

Although my primary concern has been to render as faithfully as possible the meaning and spirit of Montale's text, I felt that as a translator I had also a duty to preserve the rhythmic and idiomatic character of English. I have therefore not tried to conform to Montale's line arrangement with absolute fidelity. I say "absolute fidelity" for I have, as far as possible, attempted to do so while reproducing the maximum of the rhythmic character of the original without sacrificing the minimum of rhythm and cadence that any verse translation in English will have to have. The fact is that every line in Montale's poetry has a subtle rhythmic quality of its own which, far from being reproduced by an English line of corresponding length, is often destroyed by it. For the same reason I have ignored Montale's rhymes, puns, alliteration and assonance, for to try to render them into English is hardly the most effective way of demonstrating Montale's superb mastery, suppleness and subtlety in exploiting the whole gamut of inflections in spoken Italian.

"I have made a rule of exceptions," Montale once told me while explaining the principle governing his metrics. This led to his breaking down and regrouping traditional Italian metres — especially the hendecasyllable, the prince of Italian metres and occupying the same position in Italian poetry as blank verse does in English — in numerous fresh combinations while at the same time retaining the inflexion and structure of spoken Italian. No translation however literal, and no imitation however free, can hope to convey this quality adequately in English. And to my mind there is no virtue in trying to achieve the impossible, especially if it entails sacrificing the idiomatic naturalness of English for the sake of a jejune and unrhythmic verbal literality. I am grateful to James Laughlin and D. J. Enright for having taken the trouble of going through my translations and making many helpful suggestions.

Thanks are due to Black Sparrow Press, Los Angeles, and New Directions, New York, for letting me reprint my translations of *Xenia*, of which they brought out a limited edition of three hundred copies in 1970, and to *London Magazine*, where these and some other translations originally appeared. Thanks are also due to *The Times Literary Supplement*, *Agenda* and *Mediterranean Review* for permission to reprint some other translations which appeared there; to Yale University Press, which brought out my book *Eugenio Montale: A Critical Study of His Poetry, Prose and Criticism* (New Haven and London, 1973), where some of the translations included here appeared for the first time; to Guanda Editore, Parma, for permission to quote from Montale's preface to *Thomas Hardy: Poesie* (1968), selected and translated by me, and to Alan Ross Ltd., London, and Kentucky University Press, Lexington, Kentucky, for permission to quote from Montale's introduction to my English translation of his *Farfalla di Dinard*, brought out by them in 1970 and 1971 respectively; to Mondadori, Milan, for permission to translate from Montale's *Satura* and *Diario del '71 e del '72*, published by them in 1971 and 1973 respectively; and lastly to *The Listener* for permission to use Dr. F. R. Leavis's essay on *Xenia*.

G. S.

INTRODUCTION

by G. Singh

Although Montale's status as being, together with
Ungaretti, the most important contemporary poet in
Italy — D'Annunzio, who died in 1938, hadn't pub-
lished any significant verse since *Merope* (1911–12)
— was recognized as early as 1925, when *Ossi di
seppia* appeared, he has not only continued writing
verse during the last half century, but with the pub-
lication of each new book (*Le occasioni*, 1939; *La
bufera e altro*, 1956; *Satura*, including *Xenia*, 1971;
and *Diario del '71 e del '72*, 1973), he has added a
new dimension to his art. For each book has signalled
a new and decisive step forward, without outdating
or superseding the previous work. For one thing, the
change has been dictated by the changing social,
political and personal history reflected in his work;
for another, the poet's interest in experimenting with
a new style, diction and technique has itself entailed
that change. "An artist," Montale observes, "is a
man who works by necessity; he does not have a free
choice. In this field, more than in any other, there
exists an effective determinism. I have followed the
way imposed upon me by my times; tomorrow others
will follow different ways; I myself may change."
Together with the change dictated by the times, there
has been in Montale the desire to realize what he
considers to be "the dream of every modern poet

from Browning on," namely to forge a poetic idiom "by juxtaposing the aulic and the prosaic." ("Intentions: Imaginary Interview")

Thus in *Ossi di seppia* the crystalline hardness and precision of language is not merely the result of a reaction against D'Annunzianism, but also of an effort to renovate the language and the art of lyric poetry itself. One important element in Montale's sense of tradition has been his conviction that "after Leopardi it was almost impossible to write poetry during the rest of the century," that D'Annunzio had "experimented or touched upon all the linguistic and prosodic possibilities of our time," and that "not to have learnt anything from him would be a very bad sign." Hence in *Ossi di seppia* there are traces not only of D'Annunzio's influence, but also of Leopardi's. And yet what this book offers in its impressive coherence and totality is something quite original and characteristically Montalian. It reflects the stresses and challenges of Montale's personal life as well as those of the history of his times together with his sense of metaphysical determinism, or of what the Italian critic Alfredo Gargiulo calls "the critical corrosion of existence." The poet sets out to explore the meaning of life and all its travail and to define his sense of personal identity against the background of the Ligurian landscape and seascape, which have at once a local and a cosmic significance.

In *Le occasioni* Montale turns from the contemplation of the Ligurian landscape and what it signified to his experience of personal love, which receives an added poignancy and depth from the tragedy of the impending war. The woman loved, whom the poet calls Clizia, is both a messenger and a redeemer, a "cloud or woman, angel or petrel," and his love for her takes the form of a spiritual quest which gives both meaning and relevance to the past and the present.

The lyrics in *La bufera e altro*, on the other hand, while continuing the theme of love and war, turn, to quote Montale, "to a more direct expression and loosen the web of a too rigidly woven texture" and at the same time reflect "my historical as well as human condition." In this book a new strain emerges — the vein of religiousness which gives a particular tone and colouring to the poet's apprehension of the tragedy and futility of war as well as to his recollection of the past and his impassioned colloquy with the dead in a world which has turned into a "tormented human forest" or into a "parched land where each human/footprint seethes with blood/and lime." ("Personae separatae" and "L'arca")

But it is in *Satura*, and especially in *Xenia*, poems that Montale wrote after the death in 1963 of his wife, generally known as Mosca, that love is expressed with the frankness and familiarity of a personal attachment. Mosca's death transforms her into "a presence which is not to be put by," into someone who comes to mean "perhaps more than before." While evoking the circumstances and episodes connected with Mosca's and his own past, Montale relives them with a new intensity and crystallizes them in art. The dual realization that what he is evoking belongs irretrievably to the past, and at the same time has acquired a creative potency in memory, confers upon even the most banal and prosaic details and incidents a poignant significance.

In terms of art the result is a strikingly unique style, diction and technique for which there is no parallel in Italian poetry. And even in English the only parallel that comes to mind is the poems Hardy wrote on the death of his first wife in 1912 — poems that Montale himself, in his preface to my Italian translations of Hardy's poetry (Guanda, 1968), described as "one of the peaks of modern poetry." Nonetheless, the simplicity of tone in *Xenia* seldom borders on sentimentality, as it sometimes does in Hardy; there is little or no romantic aura about what is evoked; and instead of letting loose a flood of emotions and passions, Montale keeps them down to a remarkably low level.

Hardy's sense of bereavement as well as his recollection of the past was constantly weighed down by the feeling of what might have been; Montale's is enriched by the awareness of what was actually realized. And yet, faced with the same challenge as Hardy and at about the same point in his life and career, Montale acquits himself with superb poise, dignity and strength, both moral and artistic. The past and the present assume a new purpose as well as a renewed hold on the poet.

The poems offer a verse portrait of Mosca who is seen as both dead and alive, a portrait drawn not face to face but from various angles. On the poetic and psychological plane there is a close interfusion of what his wife was when alive and what she has come to mean after her death. Although it is always the poet who is talking, we feel that the presence of his dead wife amounts to something more than that of a merely passive listener.

It is for the most part the apparently prosaic details and events of everyday life when Mosca was alive that come back to the poet's mind, throbbing with a new life and intensity. The theme of love, however, is neither directly nor indirectly stated. In this, too, the poems differ from Hardy's. There the theme of love — whether realized or not — and the sense of regret concerning what might have been are always to the fore. In Montale, the feeling of emotional involvement rarely comes to the surface. And yet the details and associations he evokes suggest, for all their triviality, something deeper which has been left deliberately unexpressed. Thus the co-presence of Mosca before her death and after induces neither a feeling of nostalgic sentimentality nor one of regret or bitterness.

Xenia signals a new phase in Montale's poetic career. He was seventy when he wrote the sequence; the most fertile period of his creative life (although in Montale's case fertility did not mean prolificity) lay behind him. His stature as a major twentieth-century Italian poet had been amply demonstrated by his first three volumes of verse and by the impact they made on contemporary Italian poetry. With

Mosca's death he was faced with a unique challenge in both his creative and his personal life. The floods of memory and recollection were unloosed. The past acquired a new significance and a new vitality and almost completely overshadowed the present. He found himself, both poetically and existentially, in a situation where he could say with Hardy that "the past is all to him." No wonder, then, that the language of recollection in these poems is strictly and artlessly *that* and nothing more. What he recollects and what it means to him undergoes as little transformation—emotional, artistic or moral—as possible. And since Mosca's posthumous presence is always there in the guise of a mute visitor, the communion between them takes the form of an intimate monologue.

There are some other poems in *Satura* that are akin to the *Xenia* group by virtue of their style and technique. The more important among them are "A Letter," "The Last Shots," "The Ghost," "La belle dame sans merci," "The Arno at Rovezzano," "Men Who Turn Back," "Ex Voto," and the series of eight lyrics grouped under the title "After a Flight" — all included in this selection. In all these poems the subtle balance between the recollection of the past with Mosca and the realization of the present without her is achieved by means of details that are at once evocative and realistic.

The other poems in *Satura* — such as "History," "Götterdämmerung," "A Month among Children," "Words," and "Down There" — embody wit, irony and sarcasm, which represent the harvest of what Wordsworth would call the "years that bring the philosophic mind." They deal not so much with "occasions" in the Goethean sense as with prose concepts, with the result that they form a thematic link with Montale's prose work *The Butterfly of Dinard (Farfalla di Dinard)*, and even more so with *Auto da fé*. Thus the sophisticated neatness and subtlety of understatement and the undercurrent of philosophical irony one finds in some of the stories of *The Butterfly of Dinard* as well as in *Auto da fé* are also present in Montale's later poetry. In his preface to my English translation of *The Butterfly of Dinard* Montale refers to "that flexibility which too illustrious a literary tradition in the past has prevented it [Italian prose] from achieving." Montale's own successful effort in achieving that flexibility in his prose has left its mark on his later poetry as well.

T.S. Eliot defined Andrew Marvell's wit as being "something more than a technical accomplishment, or the vocabulary or syntax of an epoch; it is . . . a tough reasonableness beneath a slight lyric grace." Quite a number of poems in *Satura* and *Diario del '71 e del '72* offer, in varying degrees, a combination of interplay between "tough reasonableness" and "lyric grace" which inevitably moulds their rhythm, cadence and intonation as well as their structural pattern. And insofar as wit, epigram and irony are to some extent present even in *Ossi di seppia, Le occasioni* and *La bufera e altro*, one can say that if

Leopardi's most unique contribution to the development of Italian poetry was his invention of the philosophic lyric, that of Montale has been the modernization of post-D'Annunzian poetry in Italy — a modernization based on his interweaving within the fabric of poetry the elements of moral, intellectual and philosophic wit and irony. Such a process could not but entail the use of a crisp, ratiocinative and analytical language rather than a lyrical, melodious or sonorous one. It is a kind of diction which Pound, writing of Laforgue, called "good verbalism" as distinct not only from "lyricism and imagism" but also from bad verbalism, which meant "the use of *cliché* unconsciously, or a mere playing with phrases." For whatever puns or neologisms Montale uses, as well as his dexterous handling of internal rhymes and half rhymes, almost always presuppose a moral or intellectual need or pressure.

Hence the linguistic and stylistic innovations in Montale's later poetry are indicative as much of his creative vigour and inventiveness as of his critical awareness of the various aspects of the *Zeitgeist*. The Miltonic formula "calm of mind, all passion spent" can therefore apply only partly to the later Montale, inasmuch as his mind, far from being calm, is actively engaged in defining new areas of perception and sensibility as well as in exploring his own inner world constantly challenged by the world around him. Thus his reflections on history ("History scrapes the bottom/like a trawl net/with a jerk and more than a fish/escapes") or the twilight of the gods ("The twilight began when man/started think-ing he was/greater than a mole or a cricket"), or those on poetry (which is "rather a question/of words which are quite pressing and/in a hurry to come out of/the oven or the freezer") are all sus-tained by sardonic wit, metaphorical and imagistic inventiveness and a striking suppleness, poise and finality of diction. However subtle or profound the theme or the concept he is dealing with, Montale dis-plays a lightness of touch and a casualness of manner and approach which attest to a kind of maturity which is synonymous at once with detachment and involvement, with deliberation and spontaneity. Thus "a bird motionless on the eaves" is all, the poet tells his beloved, they can know by way of hap-piness. But it is "too expensive. It's not for us,/and he who has it doesn't know/what to do with it."

Montale is also a master of paradox. In "Before Setting Out on a Journey," for instance, he gives the idea of a journey and the precautions one takes be-fore setting out a paradoxical turn, so that it also comes to mean the last journey of one's life. "Well,/I have made extremely careful arrangements/with-out knowing anything about it./Some unforeseen event is the only/hope. But I'm told it's folly/to say so." In "Down There," while spelling out in wittily conjectural terms the shape of things to come in a more or less predictable future, he tells us how "The Creator will have little to do/if He ever had/The only saints left will be found/among dogs," but "Angels will remain/misprints that can't be deleted."

In these poems Montale both probes into the nature and meaning of reality around him and attempts, as he says in *Auto da fé* ("La solitudine dell'artista"), "to pin down the ephemeral, to render the phenomenal nonphenomenal, to make the individual 'I,' which is not so by definition, communicate — in sum, to rebel against the human condition (and thereby to assert his passionate *amor vitae*)." To his metaphysical bafflement is thus added an existential anxiety to define his personal identity, which, he says, was "doubtful from the outset," and which "the decline of values" in a commercialized culture and civilization make it all the more difficult for him to realize. For one thing the mass media render subjectivity anonymous and impersonal, so that the only individual that counts is the collective; for another, what the poet's probing into his own self yields is neither "gay nor wise nor celestial." It is only his feeling of indebtedness to Mosca — "my courage was the first/of your gifts and perhaps you didn't know it" — that sustains him in the task of self-realization. Wit and pun have a semisymbolic role, as the poet sets out to depict those who "hardly have a soul/and are afraid of losing it."

One can, therefore, say that *Satura* and *Diario del '71 e del '72* mark a distinctly decisive stage in Montale's development as a poet — development in terms of both a new sensibility and new interests. In his earlier poetry, he expressed his dreams, desires and aspirations through the figure of Clizia, who, while embodying them, also participates in the poet's sufferings and predicaments. The ethos of the last two books, on the other hand, centres upon a faith which is at once sceptical and inquisitive, hopeful and pessimistic.

It is such a faith as well as an unflagging interest in *this* world — "I love the earth, I love/him who gave it to me/him who takes it back" — which makes the poet analyse and diagnose whatever life offers him. There is something at once poetic and secular about this faith as well as about Montale's belief, as he observes in his preface to my edition of his poems in the Italian Texts Series (Manchester University Press, 1975), that "poetry has always died and has always arisen from its ashes." Even his caustic comments on certain aspects of contemporary civilization are part of his acceptance of the age in which he lives. "I accept the age in which I live. The only thing I would wish is that that rare subspecies of human beings who keep their eyes open might not become totally extinct. In the new visual civilization it is this species that is most threatened" (*Auto da fé*, "Niente paura ma . . ."). Thus Montale's all-round awareness of the problems and predicaments of our civilization conditions, as well as constitutes, his view of life and his belief that "to be alive and nothing more/is no small undertaking." Even the irony behind such drastically reductive images of life as — "we are merely the remainder/to be sold off in a clearance" or "even in a paper bag or/as a carp our pulp no longer/attracts customers" — is a typically Montalian way of expressing his faith in this life and in poetry. His muse may be "like a scarecrow/standing precariously on a chequerboard of vines," but there is no doubt as to its commitment not merely to probing and to analysing, but also to celebrating, in however oblique and ironical a way, what makes for life as well as for the life of art.

XENIA

by F. R. Leavis

Of Montale's work, it is to *Xenia* that I must confine myself, the reason being that, while I am very far from inward enough with Italian to offer myself as a critic of Italian poetry, I have been profoundly impressed by *Xenia*, and have cultivated an intimate acquaintance with it (for it really forms one poem). This special attention I have paid it is perhaps the result of a coincidence of accidents; in any case, I have found Montale's poetry peculiarly congenial. What makes it so congenial I can begin to suggest by recalling the occasion when, a couple of years ago, I had the honour, at Milan, to meet Montale. How it was that someone present came to quote from *Le Cimetière marin* I can't now remember, but Montale and I found ourselves reciting, in relays, Valéry's poem. How far we got I again can't remember, but it was plain that, between us, we could easily have reproduced the whole poem from memory.

The significance of this anecdote is not that I think Montale at all like Valéry, but the contrary. That we should both be able to recall in that way *Le Cimetière marin* seems to me, though it is Valéry's most rewarding poem, paradoxical. I have, it happens, been discussing it recently with a group of students at the University of York. Not that French literature is my business: I wanted to make and enforce some critical points in relation, in particular, to T.S. Eliot's poetry, and also to the falsities and inconsistencies of some of his most admired criticism — which his own creative practice, as exemplified compellingly in his major work, contradicts. I am thinking of the hints and formulations that were supposed to warrant his being credited with having expounded and espoused a theory of "impersonality."

Now I think that great art is necessarily impersonal, and that the true creative impersonality is what we have in the poignancy, the profound movingness, of *Xenia*. As for my "paradoxical," it registers the fact, not merely that Montale is very unlike Valéry, but that Eliot's prescription of "impersonality" goes essentially with his insistently expressed admiration for Valéry's poems — admiration which, as formulated, amounts to making the *kind* of poetry Valéry's work represents the very norm of good poetry: the kind of thing that poetry should aspire to be. In the recent discussions of *Le Cimetière marin* to which I have referred, we found ourselves agreeing that a limited judgment was decidedly called for, and that it was best put by saying that this poem was a brilliant demonstration of the poetic art conceived as a game. We had been brought to the conclusion that, for all the sonorous felicity with which the theme of death had been enunciated —

> *Ils ont fondu dans une absence épaisse,*
> *L'argile rouge a bu la blanche espèce,*
> *Le don de vivre a passé dans les fleurs!*

— the seriousness of this poetry was the seriousness of a game taken as the most important thing in life. And I produced a warrant for this formulation in what Eliot himself, quoting Thibaudet on Mallarmé in support, had written in 1924 in an introduction to *Le Serpent* (text and English translation, the poem being that which we know as *Ébauche d'un Serpent*): "To English amateurs, rather inclined to dismiss poetry which appears reticent, and to peer lasciviously between the lines for biographical confession, such an activity may seem no other than a *jeu de quilles*. But Boileau was a fine poet, and he spoke in seriousness. To reduce one's disorderly and mostly silly personality to the gravity of a *jeu de quilles* would be to do an excellent thing."

The poetry that established Eliot as a great poet doesn't answer in the least to the suggestion of this kind of sophisticated naïveté, the significance of which lies in the personal insecurity it betrays — an insecurity that plays a decisive part in his creative drive. Montale is as different from Eliot as he is from Valéry. There is no insecurity behind *Xenia*, and therefore no need for what Eliot calls "reticence." If Montale had been "reticent" in the sense enjoined by Eliot, *Xenia* could not have been written. The point I could make in my seminar was that Montale illustrates in his poem — illustrates irresistibly — the only kind of reticence that is a virtue in what offers itself as serious poetry. For him, poetry is not a *jeu de quilles* — nor is it for Eliot, but Eliot, though it is in poetry that he explores in painful earnest the meaning of life, never permits himself to recognise unequivocally the fact, nature and significance of human creativity: he is afraid. Poetry that conceives itself as a *jeu de quilles*, however strenuous, cannot be lived with; before long it becomes boring — as, I confess, for all the brilliance I have so much admired, I find *Le Cimetière marin* and *Ébauche d'un Serpent*.

For a major poet such as Montale is, poetry is one's profoundest response to experience. The theme of *Xenia* is as central, important and moving as any human theme can be, and the reticence it requires of the poet is not a refusal to recognise the full nature of what, intimately for him as sufferer, it in reality portends; but the contrary. It is the use of intelligence (and that involves the discriminations of sensibility — *l'intelligence*, I tell my students, is not the same as "intelligence") that determines how the actual pondered sense of irrevocable loss can be defined and communicated — two verbs that mean one thing to the poet. "Life" is a necessary word, but life is concretely "there" only in individual lives, and Montale's art, so different from Eliot's, as well as from Valéry's, achieves, devoted as it is to rendering with delicacy and precision his intensely personal experience, a profound and moving impersonality in the only way in which such impersonality *can* be achieved.

Professor Singh in his introduction to this book which contains the admirable translations he has done — I find his translations, which are sensitive and truly faithful in spirit, extremely helpful — makes a comparative reference to Thomas Hardy's *Veteris vestigia flammae* — the epigraph that stands in my mind for the late group of poems in which the English poet, experiencing as one thing the actual privation and the imagined presence, recalls the much loved and "much missed" woman he will never see again: "Hereto I come to view a voiceless ghost. . . ." And there is point in the comparison: a direct simplicity of personal feeling certainly relates the two poets, who in this essential characteristic differ equally from Eliot. The point, however, is inseparable from the constatation to which it leads — that of the striking unlikeness it brings out. "Simplicity," like all important words, has a range of values: Montale is immensely more subtle, more supple and more diverse than Hardy. The fact is apparent at once in the texture (hardly a felicitous metaphor — but what better is there?) and the nervous life of their verse. Hardy had to fight an unending battle against Victorian "poetic diction," and the evidence of it is there in the handful of his major victories — as, for instance, in the line I have quoted above, that which opens what seems to me his greatest poem, "After a Journey." Montale, on the other hand, is, as poetic "practitioner" (to use Eliot's favoured term), clearly a master of living — that is, today's spoken — Italian.

I say this with diffidence, though I myself don't, I regret to say, speak Italian, so that my acquaintance with the living language is sadly deficient. But my immediate responsive apprehension led rapidly to my being wholly and inexhaustibly engaged: I have read and reread *Xenia* almost daily since it arrived and find that I know it by heart; and I cannot doubt what "intuition" and sensibility tell me. There is an effect of spontaneous naturalness, going with a great range of varying inflection, tone and distance, and this effect is the product of that exquisite and sure tact which is consummate art. Montale's verse, in its sensitive precision, answers to what Blake means when he speaks of "the wiry bounding line." I had read *Xenia* through a number of times before I came to the point of telling myself that the rhymes of which I had noted (along with assonances) more at each reading insisted so little on conscious attention because of their rightness (that is, decisive inevitability) in relation to rhythm and structure. What goes with the mastery of spoken expression that makes possible the economy necessary for the essential transitions of tone is the distinctive nature of Montale's theme. Here we have the great difference between him and Hardy. If we ask (as we don't) in regard to Hardy's "woman much missed" what she was like, we can say that she was beautiful, but we have to recognise that she exists only as posited by the poet's nostalgic intensity. She is the woman with whom he was in love forty years ago. But Mosca in *Xenia* is the highly individual woman apart from whom daily life was inconceivable until the "catastrophe" of her loss, and is almost inconceivable now.

The difficulty of conceiving it as possible is marvellously conveyed by the poem, which evokes the relations between husband and wife in representative particularity. So compellingly actual is the evoked day-to-day ordinariness that one is inclined to say: "This is the art of a great novelist" (which Hardy was not). But economy of this kind is impossible in a novel — we come back to the perfection of Montale's essentially poetic technique. It is notable that, while he conveys so poignantly the inescapableness of his state of privation —

> *il desiderio di riaverti, fosse*
> *pure in un solo gesto o un'abitudine.*

> The desire to have you with me again,
> If only through a gesture or a habit.

—the focus of preoccupation for him is always Mosca herself. The "self-pity" he avows in the four lines of 7 in *Xenia I* has nothing of indulgence about it:

> *Pietà di sè, infinita pena e angoscia*
> *di chi adora il quaggiù e spera e dispera*
> *di un altro . . . (Chi osa dire un altro mondo?).*

> *'Strana pietà . . .' (Azucena, atto secondo).*

> Self-pity, infinite pain and anguish
> his who worships what's *here below*
> and hopes and despairs of something else . . .
> (And who dare say another world?)

> "Strange pity . . ." (Azucena, Act II).

The reality of *il quaggiù* that he adores is still Mosca: that is why she exists so potently for us in the poem, filling it with her unassertive presence. There is nothing assertive about Montale himself:

> *Dicono che la mia*
> *sia una poesia d'inappartenenza.*
> *Ma s'era tua era di qualcuno:*
> *era di te non più forma, ma essenza.*

> They say that mine
> is a poetry of non-belonging.
> But if it was yours, it was someone's:
> not your form any more but your essence.

His characteristic tone is given in

> *Eppure non mi dà riposo*
> *sapere che in uno o in due noi siamo una sola cosa.*

> Yet it gives me no rest to know
> that alone or together
> we are one.

I wanted earlier to say that Montale was much more sophisticated than Hardy, but hesitated because of the ambiguous force of the word in English. But I will now hazard that, in a wholly unpejorative sense, Montale — it is an aspect of his unassertiveness — is as truly sophisticated as a major artist can be. The sophistication is apparent in the wit, irony and

humour that intensify the effect of profound serious-
ness characterising his poetry. It is apparent in the
way in which he conveys his sense of the supreme
reality of Mosca. His delicate intensity of evocation
makes us feel that, in a naïve sense of "real," she is
a real presence for us — that she is really "there."
Actually, the unquestionableness of the reality he
evokes as Mosca is conditioned by his sense that
there is something at the centre of it which, though
he responds to it, can't be confidently grasped (we
recall Lawrence's insistence that the other person *is*
other). Thus the first poem of *Xenia II*, which begins
La morte non ti riguardava ("Death didn't concern
you"), closes:

Una tabula rasa: se non fosse
che un punto c'era, per me incomprensibile,
e questo punto ti riguardava.

A *tabula rasa:* except
that a point there was, though beyond my grasp,
and that point *did* concern you.

And in the second poem we have:

È strano che a comprenderti
siano riuscite solo persone inverosimili.

Strange that only
Improbable persons could understand you.

There is no nuance here of cynicism or doubting hesitance in face of the contemplated reality. In fact, Montale's communicated sense of the reality there is in experience is of an essentially fortifying kind. Two of the constituent parts of the whole poem — 13 of *Xenia I* and 13 of *Xenia II* — might seem to have the implicit function of evoking that recognition. To quote the first, which begins *Tuo fratello morì giovane:*

> *Fuori di te nessuno lo ricordava.*
> *Non ho fatto ricerche: ora è inutile.*
> *Dopo di te sono rimasto il solo*
> *per cui egli è esistito. Ma è possibile,*
> *lo sai, amare un'ombra, ombre noi stessi.*

> and no one remembered him except you.
> I asked no questions; and now it's useless.
> I'm the only one after you
> for whom he ever existed.
> But it's possible, you know, to love a shadow,
> we ourselves being shadows.

The play on *ombra* and *ombre,* which has the air of insistence, doesn't in fact at all tend to make *ombra* mere nothingness. And the other ends:

> *Coloro che hanno presunto*
> *di saperne non erano essi stessi esistenti,*
> *né noi per loro. E allora? Eppure resta*
> *che qualcosa è accaduto, forse un niente*
> *che è tutto.*

                    Those
who presumed to know it were
themselves nonexistent, as we
were for them. And so what? Yet the fact
remains that something happened, perhaps nothing
which is everything.

I prefaced the discussion of *Le Cimetière marin*
with my group of students by remarking that it was
a poem of a kind that didn't exist in English. I meant
that we had no poem answering at all to the descrip-
tion, *jeu de quilles*, which could with any plausibility
be critically offered us as major poetry. I have said at
various times to them, in my provincial way, that it
was easy to think of *Xenia*, though it was in Italian,
as an English poem. But I must confess that — as I told
them also — we have nothing like it in English.

SATURA

THE USE OF "TU"

Misled by me
the critics assert that my "tu"
is an institution, that were it not
for this fault of mine, they'd have known
that the many in me are one,
even though multiplied by the mirrors.
The trouble is that once caught in the net
the bird doesn't know if he is himself
or one of his too many duplicates.

XENIA I

1
Dear little Mosca,
so they called you, I don't know why,
this evening almost in the dark,
while I was reading Deutero-Isaiah
you reappeared beside me,
but without your glasses,
so that you could not see me,
nor could I recognize you in the haze
without that glitter.

2
Poor Mosca without glasses or antennae,
who had wings only in imagination,

a worn-out and dismantled Bible,
and not very dependable either,
night's black, a flash, a peal of thunder
and then not even the storm.
Could you have left so soon
even without talking?
But it's ridiculous to think
you still had lips.

3
At the Saint James in Paris
I shall have to ask for a "single" room
(and they don't like single guests).
And so also in the fake Byzantium
of your hotel in Venice; then immediately
to look for the girls at the switchboard,
always your friends, and leave again
the moment the automatic charge
is spent —
the desire to have you with me again,
if only through a gesture or a habit.

4
We had studied for the hereafter
a token of recognition, a whistle;
I'm now trying to modulate it in the hope
that we're all already dead without knowing it.

5
I've never understood if it was I
who was your faithful and distempered dog,

or if you were that for me.
For them you were only a myopic
insect lost in the babble
of high society. How ingenuous
of those clever people not to know
it was they who were your laughingstock,
that you could see them even in the dark,
and unmask them with your infallible flair
and your bat's radar.

6
It never occurred to you
to leave any trace of yourself
in prose or verse, which was
your charm — and then my self-disgust.
It was also what terrified me:
that you might cast me back
into the croaking mire of the neòteroi.

7
Self-pity, infinite pain and anguish
his who worships what's *here below*
and hopes and despairs of something else . . .
(and who dares say another world?)
. . .
"Strange pity . . ." (Azucena, Act II).

8
Your speech so halting and unguarded
is the only thing left
with which to content myself.

5

But the accent is changed, the colour is different.
I'm getting used to listening to you
in the tick-tack of the teletype,
or in the voluble smoke rings of
my cigars from Brissago.

9
Listening was your only way of seeing.
The telephone bill now amounts to very little.

10
"Did she pray?" "Yes, she prayed to St. Anthony
who helps one find lost umbrellas
and other things of St. Hermes' wardrobe."
"Only for this?" "Also for her dead
and for me."
"It's enough," said the priest.

11
To recall your tears (and mine were double)
is not enough to suppress your bursts of laughter.
These were like the foretaste of your private
    Last Judgment
which unfortunately never took place.

12
Spring comes out at the pace of a mole.
I shall hear you talk no more
of the poisonous antibiotics,
the rivet in your thighbone, or

the patrimony that shrewd unnamed rat
nibbled away.

Spring advances with its thick mists,
its long light days and unbearable hours.
No longer shall I hear you struggle
with the regurgitation of time
or of phantoms
or of the logistic problems of summer.

13
Your brother died young; you were
the dishevelled child who now watches me,
formally posed, from the oval of a portrait.
He wrote music but it was unpublished,
unheard, and today lies buried
in a trunk or is gone to dust.
Perhaps someone's reinventing it without knowing,
if what is written is written.
I loved him without having known him
and no one remembered him except you.
I asked no questions; and now it's useless.
I'm the only one after you
for whom he ever existed.
But it's possible, you know, to love a shadow,
we ourselves being shadows.

14
They say that mine
is a poetry of non-belonging.
But if it was yours, it was someone's:

not your form any more but your essence.
They say that poetry at its highest
glorifies the Whole in its flight,
and deny
that the tortoise is swifter than lightning.
You alone knew
that motion is not different from stillness,
that the void is the same as fullness,
that the clearest sky is but
the most diffused of clouds.
Thus I understand better your long journey
imprisoned among bandages and plasters.
Yet it gives me no rest to know
that alone or together
we are one.

XENIA II

1
Death didn't concern you.
Your dogs had also died, and the doctor
for the insane, known as crazy uncle,
your mother with her "speciality"
of rice and frogs — a Milanese triumph —
and your father who now watches me evening
    and morning
from a miniature effigy on the wall.
Yet death didn't concern you.

It was I who had to go to the funerals,
hidden in a taxi and staying aloof
to avoid tears and bother.
Even life mattered little to you,
with its fairs of vanity and greed,
and the universal gangrenes that turn
men into wolves, still less.

A *tabula rasa:* except
that a point there was, though beyond my grasp,
and that point *did* concern you.

2
You often remembered Mr. Cap (I not so much).
"I just saw him a couple of times in the bus
    at Ischia.
He's a lawyer from Klagenfurt, who sends us
    greeting cards,
and was supposed to call on us."

And at last he came; I tell him everything;
    he's stunned.
It seems a catastrophe even for him;
he's silent for a while, then mumbles something,
    rises stiffly,
bows and assures me he will send greetings.
                                Strange that only
improbable persons could understand you.
Counsellor Cap! The name's enough. And Celia?
What happened to her?

9

3

For a long time we missed the shoehorn,
the rusty tin shoehorn that had
always been with us. It seemed indecent
to introduce such a hideous object
among stuccoes and pinchbecks.
It must have been at the Danieli
that I forgot to put it back in the suitcase
or the bag. Hedia the chambermaid surely threw
    it away
into the Canalazzo. And how could I have written
to ask them to look for that trifling piece of tin?
Ours was a prestige to be saved
and Hedia the faithful had saved it.

4

Emerging cunningly
from the jaws of Mongibello
or the dentures of ice, you showed
an incredible knack for unmasking.

Mangano, the good surgeon, noticed it,
when he was exposed as the cudgel of the
    Black Shirts,
and felt amused.

Yes, that was like you: even on the verge of
    a precipice
sweetness and terror in one sole music.

5

With my arm in yours I have descended at least
    a million stairs,
and now that you aren't here, a void opens at
    each step.
Even so our long journey has been brief.
Mine continues still, though I've no more use
for connections, bookings, traps,
and the disenchantment of him who believes
that the real is what one sees.

I have descended millions of stairs with my arm
    in yours,
not, of course, that with four eyes one might
    see better.
I descended them because I knew
that even though so bedimmed
yours were the only true eyes.

6

The wine waiter poured for you a little
Inferno. And you, all fright: Must I drink it?
Isn't it enough to have been in it slowly burning?

7

"I have never been sure of being in the world."
"You don't say," you answered, "and what
    about me?"

"Oh the world, you have nibbled away at it,
if only in homeopathic doses. But I . . ."

11

8
"And Paradiso? Is there a paradise?"

"I think so, madam,
but nobody wants sweet wines any more."

9
The nuns and the widows,
death-dealing, malodorous hired mourners,
you dared not look at. Even he who has
    a thousand eyes
turns his glance away from them, you were sure.
The all-seeing he . . . since, being discreet,
you wouldn't call him god even with a small letter.

10
After a long search
I found you in a bar in Avenida
da Libertade; you didn't know
a word of Portuguese, or rather
only one word: Madeira.
And a glass of it arrived with shrimps.

In the evening I was compared to the greatest
Lusitanians with unpronounceable names
and to Carducci in addition.
Not in the least impressed,
I saw you crying with laughter, hidden
in a crowd perhaps bored but reverent.

11
Re-emerging from an infinity of time
Celia the Filipina called up
to ask about you. I think she's all right,
   I tell her,
perhaps better than before. "What do you mean?
Is she no more?" Perhaps more than before, but . . .
Celia, please try to understand . . .
                   From the other end of the wire
from Manila or some other name
in the atlas, a stutter impeded her too.
And she hung up abruptly.

12
The hawks
always too far from your sight,
you seldom saw them at close range.
One at Étretat watching its young ones'
clumsy flights. Two others
in Greece on the road to Delphi,
a mere scuffle of soft plumes and two
young, bold, harmless beaks.

You liked life torn to shreds,
life breaking out from
its unbearable web.

13
I have hung in my room the daguerreotype
of your father as a child; it's over a century old.
Lacking a pedigree of my own, so confused,

I try to reconstruct yours, but in vain.
We aren't horses and the data about our ancestors
isn't in the stud book. Those
who presumed to know it were
themselves nonexistent, as we
were for them. And so what? Yet the fact
remains that something happened, perhaps nothing
which is everything.

14
The flood has submerged
the clutter of furniture, papers, paintings,
crammed in a double-locked cellar.
Perhaps the red morocco volumes
fought blindly and so did Du Bos's
interminable dedications,
the wax seal with Ezra's beard,
Alain's *Valéry*, the original
of the *Canti Orfici*, some shaving brushes,
a thousand trifles and all
your brother Silvio's music.
Ten or twelve days in the atrocious grip
of gasoline and oil dregs. I am sure
they strove hard before losing their identity.
I, too, am encrusted up to the neck,
since my civil status was doubtful from the outset.
It isn't mud has besieged me, but the events
of an incredible reality which was never believed.
In the face of these my courage was the first
of your gifts and perhaps you didn't know it.

HISTORY

1
History doesn't unravel
like an unbroken chain
of rings.
In any case
many rings don't hold.
History doesn't contain
a before and an after:
nothing bubbles in it
on a slow fire.
It's not he who contemplates it
produces history, nor he
who ignores it. History
doesn't advance, is refractory,
detests slow change, it neither
proceeds nor recedes, it changes
track, and its direction
is not in the timetable.
History neither justifies
nor deplores,
history isn't intrinsic
for it is outside.
History doesn't administer
caresses or lashes of the whip.
History doesn't teach
anything that concerns us.
And to know all this doesn't serve
to make history more true or just.

2

Moreover, history is
not the devastating scraper some think.
It leaves underground passages, crypts,
holes and hiding-places. Some survive.
History is also benevolent: destroys
as much as it can; and were it
to destroy more it would no doubt be better,
but history is short of news,
doesn't take all its revenges.

History scrapes the bottom
like a trawl net
with a jerk and more than a fish
escapes. Sometimes one meets
the ectoplasm of someone who has escaped
and he doesn't seem particularly happy.

He doesn't know he is out, no one told him.
The others in the bag think they
are more free than he.

THE ERASER

Do you think pessimism has
really existed? If I look
around there is no sign of it.
Within us not one voice that

complains. If I cry it's a countersong
to enrich the great country of
abundance which is tomorrow.
We have scraped off with the eraser
every eruption of thought.
Now all the colours exalt
our palette except the black.

THE DEATH OF GOD

All the religions of the only God
are one: just the cooks and the cooking vary.
I was musing on this and you
interrupted me when you slipped vertiginously
down the winding stair of the Périgourdine
and split your sides with laughter.
It was a pleasant evening with just
a moment of fright. Even the Pope
said the same in Israel, but regretted it
when he was told that the great Abolished,
if ever there was one,
had expired.

IN THE SMOKE

How often I waited for you
at the station in the cold and fog,
strolled up and down, coughing, buying papers
not even worth the name,
smoking Giuba, later banned by the minister
of tobacco, what a fool!
Perhaps a wrong train, or an extra section,
or one that was simply cancelled.
I'd peer at the trolleys of the porters
to see if your luggage was there,
and you, coming late, behind it.
And there you were at last!
One memory this among many.
It pursues me in my dreams.

GÖTTERDÄMMERUNG

One reads that the twilight of the Gods
is going to begin. It's a mistake.
The beginnings are always impossible
to recognize, if
something is verified it's
transfixed by the pin.
The twilight began when man
started thinking he was
greater than a mole or a cricket.

The hell that repeats itself
is hardly the preview for a première
that was postponed long ago
because the producer was busy or ill,
or hidden who knows where,
and nobody could replace him.

TAPPING THE PHONE

I thought I was a bishop
in partibus
(the place doesn't matter, provided
it's uninhabited)
but probably I was a cardinal
in pectore
without being informed of it.
Even the Pope forgot to mention it
before he died.
Thus I can live in glory
(for what it's worth, with or without
faith in any country)
but outside of history and in civilian dress.

POETRY

1

The agonizing question
whether inspiration comes in heat or cold
doesn't belong to thermal science.
The *raptus* doesn't produce,
nor does the void conduct,
there is no poetry in sherbet or on the roasting
spit. It's rather a question
of words which are quite pressing and
in a hurry to come out of
the oven or the freezer.
Facts don't count. No sooner
do the words come out than they look around
with the air of asking themselves:
what on earth are we here for?

2

With horror
poetry rejects
the commentators' notes. But it's not certain
that the too mute
is sufficient unto itself
or to the property man who has stumbled upon it
without knowing that he is
its author.

RHYMES

Rhymes are more annoying
than the Sisters of Charity:
they keep knocking at the door and it is
impossible to dismiss them; one can
tolerate them so long as they are outside.
A decent poet gets them (the rhymes)
out of the way,
by hiding, cheating or trying to
smuggle them. But the bigots burn with zeal
and sooner or later (rhymes and old women)
knock again and they are the same as ever.

A LETTER

The old cavalry colonel
used to offer you *negroni*, *bacardi*
and the red label *röderer brut*.
He told you his name, but added
it was superfluous to remember it, and
he didn't even bother to ask yours,
still less mine. The habitués of the hotel,
though strangers, were all friends, but only
towards the last gasps of September.
Some would embrace us mistaking us for others,
and offer no apologies, but rather
would congratulate themselves on the happy error.

The big shots, the forgotten ones, would
emerge from the dark, Respighi's
widow, the heirs of Toscanini,
Tetrazzini's gravedigger, a namesake
of Malpighi's, Ramerrez-Martinelli,
a nimbus of silver hair,
and Tullio Carminati, a glory
for some surviving initiate.
(Above all the Guardian of the Keys,
an illustrious personage who thought
we were the true worthies *avant le déluge*
but it never came or was little more
than a surplus of the Acqua Alta.)
The old cavalier would always repeat
between a bourbon and a martini
that no one ever saw him beaten
at a steeplechase and conclude
by observing that rheumatism had
shorn him of his wings.
One lived among one's peers, too different
to hate each other, but too alike
in the art of keeping afloat.
The invincible *radoteur* died
some years back, perhaps before you,
and with him died the last of your suitors.
Now only package tours arrive at the hotel.
No more of the master of the liquorice
made of meconium. Nothing more
in that sewer of a canal. Not even
the band which used to honour me,
as I entered from the side of the bridge,

with the potpourri of the Guest hidden behind
    the screen:
The Count of Luxembourg.

THE LAST SHOTS

Midge or fly were names
not always consonant with
your sweet and tenacious nature.
With the help of Stanislaus we
finally settled on hellish fly.
You flew little when armoured with lime
and blackened by the smoke of an oil stove,
you were the prey of him who didn't come
and delayed the ambush. No hell
in there: only shots from Fiesole
which grazed the terrace, battery
of concert, not war. And there was
peace when you flew into a rage,
a puppet moved by a spring,
to look in the little basket for
a last dry fig.

THE GHOST

. . . .
four syllables, the name of a stranger
you never met again
and who's now dead no doubt.
A painter; he even flirted with you,
you admitted, though mildly, for he was shy.
We talked about it many years ago;
then you died and I've forgotten his name.
But here's a clandestine periodical
with faces or pictures of artists
nipped in the bud
at the outset of this century,
and there's a painting by him, quite horrible,
but then who can say? Tomorrow
it will be a masterpiece. Perhaps
you were his Clizia and did not know it.
I don't relish the idea much.
I wonder why the threads of the two spools
got so entangled; and if
that phantasm is not the lost
original and I its facsimile.

NOTHING SERIOUS

Perhaps summer has ceased to exist.
Even the cicadas have become rare. To hear one
    of them

still chirping is like a throb in the heart.
The world's crust closes, as was to be expected,
if it's a prelude to an explosion.
Even man was improbable, they say.
I don't know for whose benefit at the lottery
the number that never came out before
was extracted up there.

But there won't be an explosion. Enough
to have something worse
which is infinite by nature while
the better doesn't last long.
The Trimurtic Sybil exorcises
the Fates, breathing life into the stillborn.
Only he is dead who thinks
of the cicadas. And if he isn't aware of this,
the fault is his own.

TIME AND TIMES

There isn't one unique time: many
tapes run parallel, but
often in opposite directions,
and they rarely intersect.
But when they do the sole
truth comes out which is
no sooner revealed than cancelled
by him who supervises the gears
and switches. And one falls back into

the unique time. But in that instant
only the few who are living
have recognized themselves to say
good-bye, not *au revoir*.

I SEE A BIRD

I see a bird motionless on the eaves,
it could be a pigeon but is thinner
and has a little tuft; or perhaps
it's the wind, who knows, the windows
are shut. If you also see it, when awakened
by the outboard motors, this is all
one can know by way of happiness.
It's too expensive. It's not for us,
and he who has it doesn't know
what to do with it.

LA BELLE DAME SANS MERCI

To be sure the cantonal seagulls
waited in vain for the crumbs
I used to throw on your balcony,
that you might hear their cries even when asleep.

Today neither of us turns up for the appointment,
our breakfast grows cold among piles
of my useless books and your various relics:
calendars, jewel cases, medicine
bottles and creams.

Your astounding face lingers still,
carved against the morning's chalky
background; but a life without wings
can't reach it and its suffocated fire
is no more than the flash of a lighter.

HERE AND THERE

We have long been rehearsing the performance,
but the trouble is we aren't always the same.
Many have already died, others change
sex, beards, faces, age
or language. For years (or centuries)
we've been rehearsing the parts, the long tirade,
or merely "dinner is served,"
nothing more. For millennia we have
been waiting for someone to greet us
on the stage with applause, or even
with hissing — it doesn't matter — provided
a *nous sommes là* is there to console us.
Unfortunately we don't think in French,
and so we are always on this side, never on that.

I FEEL REMORSE FOR HAVING CRUSHED

I feel remorse for having crushed
the mosquito on the wall,
the ant on the pavement.
I feel remorse but here I am in a dark suit
for the meeting or the reception.
I feel sorrow for everything, even
for the slave who advises me on life's
    various activities,
for the beggar to whom I don't give alms,
for the madman who presides over
the administrative council.

A MONTH AMONG CHILDREN

Children play
the newest games,
dull abstruse ramifications
of the game of goose.

Children hold our future
in their hands.
Not these who toss it about,
but the far-off generations.

This fact is not important,
nor are the ancestors even.

What they have at their feet is the present
and that's more than enough.

Children have no love for God,
no opinions.
If they discover salami, they reject
milk and pap.

Children are tender and
cruel. They don't know the difference
that there is between a body
and its ashes.

Children don't love nature
but they use it. They pitch
tents among the pines,
and swarm like bees.

Children don't prick
but smash. They sprout like elves,
and thread their way
through the narrowest interstices.

Children can put up only
with old men and women. Climbing
into their laps they snatch
brooches, pendants, tufts of hair.

Children are happy
as never before.
They appear in glossy periodicals
in the ads for washing machines.

Children don't ask themselves
if there is another Life.
And they're right. That hard core
is not pumpkin seeds.

Children . . .

ON THE GROUND FLOOR

We discovered that the porcupine liked
spaghetti al ragú. It would come
late in the night, and we
would leave the dish on the kitchen floor.
It kept its young sheltered near
the wall of the garage. They were
very small and curled up. That they
were indeed so many not even
the watchman who was always tipsy
could be sure. Later on the porcupine
was seen in the policemen's kitchen garden.
We did not realize that
there was an opening among the creepers.

LATE IN THE NIGHT

One can't converse with shades
on the phone.
During our mute dialogues there is
no microphone boom or loudspeaker.
However, even words serve
when they don't concern us, picked up
by mistake by a telephone operator
and relayed to someone who
isn't there, doesn't hear.
Once they came from Vancouver
late in the night while I was waiting
for a call from Milan.
At first I was taken aback,
but then hoped that the mix-up would continue.
One voice from the Pacific, the other
from the lagoon. At that time
the two voices talked freely as never
before. Then nothing happened,
we assured the operator that
everything was perfect, in order,
and could continue, in fact *must* continue.
Nor did we ever know who'd foot the bill
for that miracle.
But I didn't remember a single word.
The time zone was different, the other
voice wasn't there, and I
wasn't there for her, even the languages
got mixed up, a hotchpotch of jargons,
curses and laughter. By now

after all these years
the other voice has forgotten and perhaps
thinks I'm dead. I think
it's she who is dead, but was
alive for a second at least,
and did not know it.

WORDS

Words
if they awaken
reject the most propitious
place for them,
the rag paper from Fabriano,
ink from China, the binding
of leather or velvet
which keeps them secret.

Words
when they wake up
recline on the backs
of vouchers, on the margins
of lottery tickets,
on wedding cards or those
of condolence;

words
ask for nothing better

than the tangle of keys
in the portable Olivetti,
the dark little pockets
of the waistcoat or the bottom
of the wastepaper basket; reduced
to crumpled bits of paper.

Words
are not at all happy
to be thrown out
like whores and received
with a furore of clapping
and shame.

Words
prefer slumber
in a bottle to the mockery
of being read, sold,
embalmed and put into hibernation;

words
are everyone's property and in vain
do they hide in dictionaries,
for there's always a rogue
who digs up the rarest
and most stinking truffles;

words
after an eternal wait
give up the hope
of being pronounced

once and for all
and then die with him
who possessed them.

THE END OF 1968

From the moon or thereabouts
I've observed the tiny planet
that contains philosophy, theology, politics,
pornography, literature and the sciences,
occult or otherwise;
man too (including myself),
and it's all very strange.

A few hours and it will be midnight and the year
will end with the popping of champagne
corks and the explosion of firecrackers,
bombs too or worse, but not
where I am. It doesn't matter
if someone dies, so long as nobody knows him,
and so long as he's far away.

UNKNOWN DIVINITIES

They say
that of the terrestrial divinities amongst us

one meets increasingly fewer.
Many people doubt they even
exist on this earth.
They say
that in this world or above
there's only one of them or none at all;
they think
that the ancient sages were all mad,
slaves of witchcraft, if they held
that some divinity, incognito,
visited them.

I say
that I've seen them more than once,
that immortals who are invisible
to others and perhaps unaware
of their privilege,
deities in jeans with rucksacks,
priestesses in overcoats and sandals,
Pythias wrapped up in the smoke
of a huge bonfire of pine cones,
numinous phantoms but not unreal,
tangible though never touched,
but I was too slow to try to unmask them.

They say
that the gods don't come down here,
that the creator doesn't descend with a parachute,
that the founder doesn't found because
no one has ever founded or fused him,
and we are merely miscarriages

35

of his nullifying potency;
yet
if one divinity, even of the lowest rank,
has grazed me, that thrill
revealed everything to me,
though I could not recognize it
and the beingless being vanished.

THE BLACK ANGEL

O great fuliginous angel
shelter me
under your wings,
that I may graze the spikes
of the thornbush, the illuminations of the ovens
and kneel down on the extinguished
embers in case some fringe
of your feathers may still be there

O little black angel,
neither celestial nor human,
who shines through changing colours
formless and multiform, equal
and unequal in the swift lightning
of your mysterious confabulation

O black angel unveil
yourself but do not kill me

with your splendour, nor dispel
the mist that haloes you, stamp
yourself on my thought, for no eye
can resist your dazzle,
coal-black angel who hides
under the shawl of the roast chestnut vendor

great ebony angel,
dark or white,
if being tired of my wanderings I
were to pull your wing and hear it
creak
I wouldn't be able to recognize you,
as I do now, in sleep, half-awake
in the morning, for between the true
and the false not one needle's eye
can hold the biped or the camel,
and the burnt residue, the grime
that remains on the fingertip is
less than the fine dust of your
last feather, great angel of ashes
and smoke, mini-angel chimney sweep.

THE ARNO AT ROVEZZANO

Big rivers are the image of time,
cruel and impersonal. Seen
from a bridge they declare their inexorable

nullity. Only the hesitant
bend of some marshy reed-bed,
some mirror gleaming amid
brushwood and moss can reveal
that the water becomes aware of itself like us
before turning into vortex and plunder.
So much time has passed,
yet nothing has changed since when
I'd sing to you on the phone
"toi qui fais l'endormie"
amid immoderate peals of laughter.
Your house was a lamp seen from
the train. It leans over the Arno
like the Judas tree which wanted to protect it.
Perhaps it's still there, or there
only in ruins. Full of insects,
you would tell me, and quite uninhabitable.
Other comforts are our lot now, other
discomforts.

WE WENT

We went for mushrooms
on the carpets of moss
under the chestnut trees.

We went for crickets
and the fireflies were
our lanterns.

We went for lizards
and I
never killed one.

We walked on the ants
and I always
avoided trampling on them.

We went to the elementary school,
to the primary cramming,
the secondary, tertiary and mortuary.

We took wrong paths
and I've never been
a collector of them.

We went for the messtin,
for something to do,
for bad luck, for vigilance and
for misadventure.

We no longer went for mushrooms
but for the far-off epochs
of a safer age
or rather for no age at all
since there was no keyhole in
the lock.

MEN WHO TURN BACK

Maybe
you no longer are what you have been
and rightly so. The sandpaper
has duly scraped and on us
each line gets thinner.
Yet something was written on the pages of our life.
To hold them up against the light is to magnify
        that sign,
to form a hieroglyph bigger than the diadem
that used to dazzle you.
No more will you emerge from the hatch
of the hovercraft or from the seaweed's depth
— skindiver of muddy rapids —
to give meaning to the meaningless. You will walk
up the escalators of Mercury's temples,
the only living person among
masked corpses, and will not ask me
if it was an illusion, choice or message,
and which of us was the bull's eye they shoot at
with an arrow in the fairground booths.
Nor do I ask myself.
I am one who has seen for an instant,
and that's enough for one walking in file,
as it happens with us now if we are still alive,
or delude ourselves we are. Everything's slipping.

EX VOTO

It happens
that the spirit's affinity may
fall short of words and gestures,
but diffuse like magnetism — something
rare, but it happens.

It may well be
that only distance and oblivion
are real, that the dry leaf is
more real than a green shoot. This
and much more, may well be.

I quite understand
your obstinate wish to be always
absent, for only thus
can your magic be revealed. Your innumerable tricks
I quite understand.

I will
insist on looking for you in the twig, never
in the full-grown tree; in the void
but not in fullness; in that
which even resists the drill.

It was, or it wasn't
the will of the gods who preside
over your far-off hearth, strange, multiform,
multispirited pets;
perhaps it was as it seemed to me,
or it wasn't.

I do not know
if my nonexistence soothes
your destiny, or if yours
overflows mine, if innocence is a fault,
or if one learns on the threshold of your home.
All this about you, about me,
I know, and I do not know.

BEFORE SETTING OUT ON A JOURNEY

Before setting out on a journey
one examines timetables, connections, stops,
overnight stays, reservations
(of rooms with bath or shower,
one- or two-bed rooms, even a suite);
one consults
the Hachette guides and the museum
guides, changes money, sorts out francs
from escudos, rubles from kopecks;
before the journey one informs
friends or relatives, checks
suitcases and passports, completes
the outfit, acquires an additional
quantity of razor blades, and finally
gives a glance at the will, a pure
superstition this, since the percentage
of air disasters is nil;
                        before

a journey one is calm, but suspects
that the wise don't travel and that
the pleasure of returning is a costly one.
And then one leaves and everything's
O.K. and all's for the best
and useless.
. . . .
                        As to *my* journey? Well,
I have made extremely careful arrangements
without knowing anything about it.
Some unforeseen event is the only
hope. But I'm told it's folly
to say so.

THE SEASONS

My dream is not in the four seasons.

Not in winter
that drives us close to the worn-out
radiators and sprinkles with icicles
hair already grey,
nor in the bonfires lit by vagabonds
in the suburbs, nor in the smoke
of hell that laps the eaves,
nor even in the Christmas tree
which survives, perhaps, only in prisons.

My dream is not in spring,
the age fabled by the ancients, nor
in the cuttings that find it hard
to put forth new shoots, nor
in the marmot's trilling chirp
as it peeps out of its hole,
nor even in the opening of taverns and wine cellars
under the illusion that it will no longer rain
or will rain elsewhere perhaps, who knows where.

My dream is not in summer
neurotic with false mirages and lunations
of ill-omen, nor in the black puppet
of a scarecrow, nor in the tangle
of dragnets torn by dolphins,
not in the sultry glare of its mornings,
nor in the underwater journeying of him
who drowns with himself and his past.

My dream is not
in the misty, wine-red autumn
found only in the calendars or the almanacs
of Barbanera, nor in its black short evenings,
in the harvest time or liturgical processions,
in the cry of the peacocks and the turning
        of the oil mills,
nor in the obstructing of the larva
        and the dormouse.

My dream never rises from the womb
of the seasons, but in timelessness

which lives where reasons die
and God alone knows if it was
time or if it was useless.

AFTER A FLIGHT

1
Thick birches hid the sanatorium
where someone sick from too much
love of life, and hovering
between all and nothing was feeling
bored. A cricket provided by the clinic
was chirping with the cuckoo you had already
heard in Indonesia at lesser cost.
There were the birches, a Swiss nurse, three
or four madmen in the courtyard, an album
of exotic birds, the telephone
and some chocolates on the bedside table.
And, of course, I too was there
with other bores to give you comfort
such as you could have given us in plenty
if only we'd had eyes. I had.

2
Your pace isn't priestly, you
haven't learnt it abroad, at the school
of Jaques-Dalcroze — it's more affectation
than a ritual. It came from Oceania

with some fish bones in the heel.
Relatives, physicians, assistant physicians
noticed it without knowing that the coral reefs
are not Le Focette, but the foam
of the hereafter, the exit from the present.
Three bones in your foot, not three
fins of a shark which are edible.
Then came an artificial sleep
to engulf you. Now only your whisper
in the long-distance call with its complicated
code and the complaints of other callers.
Nothing else from the wire,
not even a light furtive step
on the carpet. An aquarium's sleep.

3
If, swept by a vortex, you
had reached the vegetable ganglions
where the Amerinds, those celestials,
weave themselves tighter and tighter
in order to flee the white man,
they'd have garlanded you with percussive homage
even though you haven't the long
slit eyes of the Mongolian women.
Their flight took so long; many
generations to be sure. Your own
was brief and saved you from the darkness
or from the claw that held you hostage.
Now one no longer needs
the telephone in order to hear you.

4
My road passed
indiscriminately through gods and demons.
All a changing of masks and beards,
a Volapük, a Guaranì, and a sharp
Charabia that nobody could understand.
Now don't ask why I identified you with that face,
or that sound with which you entered into a head
deafened by too many klaxons.
Some bond or noose has also reached me
of which you obviously know nothing. At first
your head seemed to evaporate and mine
was no better. You threw a glass from the window,
then a shoe and you might almost have thrown
    yourself
had I not been by your side and watching you.
But you know nothing about this; it's useless
to ask if it was a dream, a noose or a trap.
Surely your road too went through hell,
and it was like bidding adieu
to an uninhabitable Elysium.

5
While I think of you the pages of the calendar
rapidly fall off. Bad weather
this morning, and Time even worse.
The best of you exploded among mastic trees,
blackberries, streams, the croaking
of frogs and the short flights of stilt-birds
unknown to me (the Cavaliers of Italy,
as they are called!) and I lay sleepless

amidst the mouldy smell of books and ledgers.
The worst of me also exploded:
the desire to retrace the years
and beat fleet-footed Time
with a thousand tricks.
They say that I believe in nothing
if not in miracles.
I don't know what you believe,
whether you believe in yourself or let
others see and create you.
But this is more than human, it's the privilege
of him who sustains the world
and does not know it.

6

On reaching Sant'Anna, the village
of the Nazi massacre, on which
a peak suddenly gravitates, I saw you
climb to the top like a roebuck
beside a slender Polish woman,
and the water rat, your guide, most
ibexlike of all.
I waited five hours in the square,
counting the names of the dead on the monument
and including myself among them *ad honorem*
for a joke. In the evening the outboard motor
jolted us into the Burlamacca,
a dam of excrement on which there pours out
boiling water as if from an oil well.
Perhaps a preview of hell.
The Burlamacchi, Caponsacchi . . . spectres
of heresy and of unreadable poems.

Poetry and the sewer, two
inextricable problems (but
I didn't talk to you about this).

7
A slow receiver of neologisms
in the drowsiness of early morning
I wasn't sure whether the name of the flying machine
by which I wanted to reach you furtively
was Hovercraft or Hydrofoil.
In the meantime you had fled with a smart water rat
nimbler than I and alas a good deal younger.
I wandered round lazily all day,
reflecting that between Lear and Cordelia
such thoughts didn't run,
and hence not even the remotest
comparison was possible. I came back
with the group after visiting the tombs
of Lucumos, dens of aristocrats
disguised as thieves, the prisonlike street
à la Piranesi in old Leghorn.
I threaded through the tunnels of rubbish.
The sky was marvellous, almost
horrific when I returned. Even the link
with the tragedy went up in smoke,
for on top of everything I
am not even your father.

8
I cannot breathe if you are far away —
thus Keats to Fanny Brawne whom
he saved from oblivion.

It's strange — *si parva licet* —
that I cannot say the same.
I can breathe much better if you are
away. Nearness brings back to us
memorable events: but not
as they happened, foreseen by us
as future smelling salts,
if needed, or thieves' vinegar
— (now nobody faints for such trifles,
as a broken heart). It's the mass
of facts on which the impact falls,
and the dead woman being present,
the planking doesn't hold.
I won't try to discuss it with you.
I know that if you read me you'd think
that you have given me the necessary propellent,
and the rest (so long as it *isn't*
silence) matters little.

TWO VENETIAN PIECES

I
From the windows I could see the typists.
And down below, the blind alley,
with the smell of fried scampi, the nauseating
stench from the canal. What a treat
to look at that landscape in Venice
and she having come from afar.

She who loved only Gesualdo,
Bach and Mozart and I
a horrible operatic repertoire
with some preference for the worst.
Then to complicate matters there was
the clock that showed five o'clock
when it was only four,
our rushing out, Saint Mark's, the deserted
Florian, Riva degli Schiavoni,
the trattoria Paganelli
recommended by some stingy Tuscan painter,
two rooms that didn't even communicate,
and the next day, seeing you pass by
without so much as casting a glance
at my Ranzoni. I wondered who was absent-minded,
I or she or both, but kept following
a railroad track that was opposite, not parallel.
And to think that we had conjured up
such beautiful images on the steps
leading from the Oltrarno to the big square.
But then we were there strolling among the pigeons
and photographers in the bestial heat,
carrying the heavy catalogue of the
        Biennial Exhibition,
which was never consulted and which
wasn't easy to get rid of. We came back
by the boat, stepping over birdseed,
buying souvenirs, post cards and sunglasses
at the stalls. I think it was in '34
and we were too young or too strange
for a city that demands tourists and old lovers.

II

Farfarella the garrulous porter,
faithful to his orders, says
that he isn't allowed to disturb
the lover of bullfights and safaris.
I beg him to try and tell him
I'm a friend of Pound's (I exaggerated
a little) and deserve special treatment.
Who knows . . . He picks up the receiver,
talks, listens, talks again
and Hemingway the bear takes the bait.
He's still in bed,
from his hairy face only his eyes
and the marks of eczema stand out.
Two or three empty bottles of Merlot,
avant-garde of the gallons that are to come.
Down in the restaurant they are all at table.
We don't discuss him, but our very dear friend
Adrienne Monnier, rue de l'Odéon,
Sylvia Beach, Larbaud, the roaring 'thirties
and the braying 'fifties. Paris,
London, a pigsty, New York
stinking, pestiferous. No more
hunting in the marsh, no more
wild ducks, no more girls, not even
the idea of a book along these lines.
We make out a list of mutual friends,
whose names I don't know. Everything's rotten,
decayed. Almost in tears he asks me
not to send him people of my kind,
especially if they are intelligent.

Then he gets up, wraps himself in a bathrobe,
and shows me to the door with an embrace.
He lived for a few more years
and, dying twice, had occasion
to read his obituary.

THE REPERTORY

The repertory
of memory is worn out,
like a suitcase
that has borne the labels of so many hotels
with one or two stickers still left
which I daren't take off. Porters, night doormen
and taxi drivers will see to that.

The repertory of your memory
you yourself passed on to me
before leaving. There were names
        of various countries,
dates of stays and a blank page at the end
with dotted lines . . . as if to suggest,
were it ever possible, "continued."

The repertory
of our memory can't be imagined
cut in two by a blade.
It's one page only with marks

of stamps, erasures, some bloodstains.
It wasn't a passport or a testimonial.
To use — even hope to use it —
would still mean life.

DOWN THERE

The earth will be supervised
from astral platforms

Massacres will become more probable
or less down there

Prophets will disappear; prophecies
too, were there any

I You We will go
out of use

To say birth death end beginning
will all be one

To say yesterday or tomorrow
an abuse

To hope — a *flatus vocis* nobody
understands

The Creator will have little to do
if He ever had

The only saints left will be found
among dogs
. . . .

Angels will remain
misprints that can't be deleted.

GENIUS

Genius unfortunately doesn't
speak through its own mouth.

Genius leaves few traces of its footsteps
like a hare on the snow.

The nature of genius is such
that the moment it stops walking all the gears
are paralysed.

And the world stops, waiting for a hare
to run across
improbable snowfalls.

Firm and swift in its dance
it can't read marks

long since pulverised,
indecipherable.

REBECCA

Each day I discover more and more
that I am wrong: the total is missing.
The addenda are all right, perfect,
but the sum? Rebecca watered her camels
and drank herself.
I attend to the pen and the soup plate
for myself and for others.
Rebecca was thirsty, I hungry,
but we cannot be absolved.
There wasn't much water in the wadi, just
        a few puddles,
and in my kitchen very little wood to burn.
Yet we tried for ourselves and for others
in the smoke and the mud with some living
bipeds or even quadrupeds.
O meek Rebecca whom I have never met!
Just a handful of centuries divides us,
a blink of the eye for him who understands
        your lesson.
Only the divine is total in the sip
and the crumb. Only death triumphs if
you want the whole portion.

IN THE SILENCE

Today there's a general strike,
and no passer-by in the street.
Only the sound of a radio from the other
side of the wall. Of late
somebody must have come to live here.
I wonder what will happen to production.
Even spring is slow in producing itself.
They have turned off the radiators early
and realized that the postal system is useless.
There's no great harm if normal
activities are delayed.
It's natural that some gears should fail to work.
Even the dead have started agitating.
They too form part of the total
silence. You lie under a tombstone.
There's no use awaking you,
for you are always awake. Even today
in this universal sleep.

LIGHTS AND COLOURS

Whenever you appear
it's always in the red bed-jacket,
with your eyes rather swollen like those
of one who has seen.
These mute visitations of yours

seem quite inexplicable.
Perhaps it's only a glitter from your spectacles,
almost a flash from a mirror
which cuts across the mist. Last time
it was an apricot-coloured worm hobbling
uncomfortably on the bedside carpet.
It wasn't easy to make it glide up
a piece of paper and throw it
alive in the courtyard. You yourself
would weigh no more.

THE OTHER

I don't know who may have noticed it,
but our dealings with the Other were one
long subterfuge. To publicize them
would be to beseech clemency, more
than showing obsequiousness. It isn't
our fault that we weren't he;
nor his fault or merit that we
have the appearance we have.
There is even no fear.
The shrewd flamingo hides
its head under its tail and imagines
that the hunter cannot see it.

DIARIO DEL '71

TO LEONE TRAVERSO

I
When possessed by the devil a woman
plays hide and seek it's difficult to catch her
by the hair because of the *toupet*.

And it's no use one's letting oneself go
with the current as Goethe the neoterist tried to do.

Musty in-folios with tapes and studs
don't conform to his wishes or rarely.

Yet you met poetry in all its forms,
you moth-eaten, yes, but always
ravished and then burnt by life.

II
I too dreamt I'd be one day
mestre de gai saber, but it was
a vain hope. A dried up laurel
doesn't put forth leaves even for the roast.
With maladroit fingers I try to play
on the celesta or the pestles of the vibraphone,
but the music keeps receding. And anyway
it wasn't the music of the spheres . . . What I knew
was never gay nor wise nor celestial.

POOR ART

The painting
on the easel demands sacrifices of him
who paints it and even more of him who buys it
and doesn't know where to hang it.
For some years I have only painted decoys
and birds caught in sacks
on blue sugar bags or wrapping paper,
with wine and coffee for the colours
and smears of toothpaste if the background
was a tasseled sea. I also composed
with ashes and the dregs of cappuccino
at Sainte-Adresse where Jongkind found
his frozen lights and the packet
was protected by cellophane and camphor
(without much success).
This is the part of me that has managed to survive
of the nothing that was in me and
of everything that you were without knowing it.

CHANGING COLOUR

She took life with a small spoon
being
thoroughly *outside it* and elusive.

An embarrassed girl, early married
to a real and imperfectible
nobody.

She had another husband who gave her
a status and took her
to the Lebanon as his useful travel kit.

But she missed the travel agency
where someone found her
who was not less selenite but understandable.

It was in the interval between her two husbands,
an air reservation and a word
was enough.

The man brought her back to her succulent
paternal language and he
didn't even ask what he got.

In the Lebanon one lives as if the world
didn't exist, almost more buried
than the cedars under the snow.

She remembers it in various languages,
a barbarous cocktail of borrowings,
he supposes her Arabized and docile
to the feasts and jeers of the Celestials.

He sees himself in slippered feet,
prostrate on the carpets of innumerable
mosques and his gaze is illumined

by the stones that change colour,
the alexandrites, the chameleonites
which she bought at a low price in the bazaars.

But she herself was priceless, and so was he,
while looking for a travel agency
near Marble Arch.

He was a rentable man, devoid
of any attributes, but ready
to receive one. And now that he has got it,
he thinks it's enough. And she?
Happily she doesn't know. He
who gives light risks the darkness.

THE POSITIVE

Let's prostrate ourselves at sunrise
and let everyone turn toward his Mecca.
If something still remains, even a bare
yes, let's say it with closed eyes.

THE NEGATIVE

Like yokes of a single egg
the young enter the gymnasium of life.

Venus guides them, Mercury
divides them and Mars will do the rest.
The light of this still timid
spring will not shine for long
on the Acropolis.

TO C.

One day we tried to find a *modus moriendi*
which was neither suicide nor survival.
Others took the initiative for us;
and now it's too late to dive again
from the rock. That life itself
in its diapason was an evil spirit
you never could believe: the hours
followed one upon the other, pride
was enough for you, and for me
the niche of the bird-feeder.

RED ON RED

It's almost spring and already
the flower clusters climb to the window
overlooking the courtyard. There will soon
be a siege of leaves and ants.
A beetle tries to cross my tax records,

red on red. I wish
it could also discolour the contents.
The bell has struck midday, a telephone
rings, and the radio announces
two hundred dead on the autostrada,
an Easter record.

THE KINGFISHER

They say
that the King of fishers only looks
for souls.

I have seen more than one
bring to the slime of the pools
flashes of lapis lazuli.

His kingdom is measured in millimetres,
his elusive arrow
by flashes.

Only the Kingfisher has
a just measure,
the others hardly have a soul
and are afraid of losing it.

IN THE COURTYARD

In the indolent spring with the holidays
at hand, the city empties itself.
And since the Ides of March a blackbird
has been sitting on the window sill, pecking
at grains of rice and crumbs.
There's no point in its going down into
the courtyard, packed with cars,
cases, bags and tennis rackets.
At the window in front one can see
an antiquarian in a dressing gown and
two Siamese cats. From another vantage point
a red-faced boy shoots at the pigeons
with his gun. The spacious apartment
of the great Oncologist is always dark
        and deserted.
But it wasn't so one night when it became
ablaze with lights at the news
that the aforesaid had been elected to parliament.
And there was so much uncorking of champagne,
camera flashes, laughter and congratulations
that even Gina was awakened and ran
all excitement to tell me: he has made it!

HIDING PLACES

When I'm not sure of being alive
the certainty is only a few steps away,

and yet it takes an effort
to find such objects as a pipe,
my wife's little wooden dog, her brother's
obituary, three or four
pairs of her glasses, the cork
of a bottle that long ago
struck her on the forehead at the New Year's
cotillion at Sils Maria
and other baubles. They change lodgings,
get into the most hidden nooks,
risk ending up in a dustbin at any moment.
They've formed a conspiracy to sustain me,
for they know better than I
the thread that binds them to him
who'd like to, but dares not get rid of them.
In later years the automatic Gubelin
will try to join them, but will always be rejected.
We bought it at Lucerne and she said
that it rains too much at Lucerne and that
it would never work. And in fact . . .

EL DESDICHADO

I'm following on television Karajan's *Carmen*
carefully boned and too sugary.

Brick-coloured stuffed envelopes piled
on the table capture shouts and lamentations.

With the movable lampshade I turned
a ray of light on it, then turned it off.

Don't expect tears or help from me, brothers.
If I could line up with you, I'd ask
for the alms of a word you can't give me,
for you know only the cry, a cry
that dies down in the stinking air,
merges with it and doesn't speak.

RECEDING

The wood worm was born I think
in a cabinet I saved from removals
and floods. It drills very slowly
and its microsound is incessant.
It has probably fed for months
on the dust — the fruit of its labour.
One might say it ignores my existence,
but I know about it.
I myself have been drilling unawares
a stump which I do not know
and which someone watches, annoyed
by the chirping it causes, someone
who in turn keeps drilling, unconscious
of his drilling, and so on
in a long telescope of pieces
one inside the other.

MY MUSE

My Muse is far away: one might say
(and most do) that she never existed.
If indeed there was one, she dresses like a scarecrow
standing precariously on a chequerboard of vines.

She flutters as best she can;
she has resisted the monsoons, staying
upright, though somewhat stooped.
If the wind drops she can still
move almost as if to tell me:
walk without fear, so long
as I can see you I'll give you life.

My Muse has long since left
the theatrical costumer's storeroom
and he who dressed up in her
was a high class person. One day
she was filled with me and walked
proudly. Now she still has a sleeve with which
she conducts her quartet of straws.
It's the only music I can bear.

WHERE CHARITY BEGINS

This violent gust of charity
which beats down upon us is
a last imposture.

It will never begin at home
as they taught us at Berlitz; nor
will it ever be found in the school readers.

And certainly not with you, Malvolio,
nor with your gang, nor with the peals of a trumpet,
nor with him who turns it into a second
skin and then throws it away.

Charity belongs to no one.
It's like the soap bubble that shines for an instant,
then bursts and doesn't know who blew it.

THE FIRE

It is Pentecost and there's no way
for tongues of fire to descend
from heaven. And yet a Jeremiah
who appeared on the television said
that it could happen any time.
There is no fire to be seen, only
some smoke bombs at the corner of Via Bigli.
Those madmen in double-breasted coats
or cassocks don't seem to be
well informed about their deathly appearance.
The fire doesn't come from on high
but from down below, it has never been
either extinguished, or grown,
no one has ever seen it,

neither fireman nor vulcanologist.
Whoever sees it doesn't give
the alarm but keeps quiet. One
no longer believes in birds of ill omen.

THE SWALLOW

The swallow lying curled up on the pavement
had its wings encrusted with tar
and it could not fly. Gina,
who tended it, loosened the clots
with cotton wool soaked in oil
and perfume; she combed its feathers
and hid it in a little basket just
big enough for it to breathe in.
It looked at her almost gratefully
with only one eye. The other
didn't open.
It ate half a leaf of lettuce
and two grains of rice, then slept
for a long time. The following day at dawn
it flew off without saying good-bye.
The maid on the floor above saw it.
What a hurry it was in, was the comment.
And to think that we had saved it from the cats.
But perhaps now it can look after itself.

AT THIS POINT

Stop at this point
says the shadow.
I have accompanied you in war and in peace
and also in the interval.
I have been for you both excitement and boredom,
have inspired you with virtue you didn't
possess, with vices you didn't have.
If now I leave you alone
you won't be hurt, you'll be lighter
than leaves, mobile as the wind.
I must raise the mask, I am your thought,
I am your "un-necessary," your useless exterior.
At this point stop, get away from my breath
and run through the sky like a rocket.
There is still some light on the horizon
and whoever sees it is not
a madman, but only a man
and you thought that you weren't one,
for the love of a shadow.
I have deceived you but now at this point
I say to you stop.
Neither your worst nor your best
belong to you and as for what you will have
you can do without a shadow.
At this point look with your eyes
and also without eyes.

I NEVER TIRE OF TELLING

I never tire of telling my trainer,
throw in the sponge,
but he doesn't hear me
for he has never been seen in the ring
or even outside it.
Perhaps in his way he tries
to save me from dishonour,
and maybe he takes such care of me,
idiot or buffoon that I am,
that he holds me in balance between rage
        and gratitude.

THE FIRST DAYS OF JULY

The first days of July are here
and already thought
has entered the moratorium.
There are no dramas,
only disorders.
That the mind's rhythm is slowing down creates
inexplicably serious problems.
It's better to face time when it's crowded,
half a day is enough to pass it.
But now in the first days of July
every second drips and the plumber
is on holiday.

LEAVE-TAKING

Let my valediction descend on you
Chiliasts, friends! I love the earth, I love

him who gave it to me

him who takes it back.

DIARIO DEL '72

THE SMELL OF HERESY

Was Miss Petrus, the hagiographer and secretary
of Tyrrell, also his mistress?
Yes, was the answer of the Barnabite,
and a shiver of horror ran through the relatives,
friends and other casual guests.

I was still a child and indifferent
to the matter. The Barnabite was
also a tolerably good pianist
and with four hands, or perhaps four feet,
we sang or rather ground out
In questa tomba oscura
and other such pleasantries.

That he smacked of heresy even
his relatives didn't seem to know.
When he was dead and already forgotten
I learned that he was suspended *a divinis*
and I remained agape with astonishment.
Suspended yes, but by whom? From what
and why? Was he attached in mid-air
to a string? And was the divine
a hook from which one is suspended?
Can one sniff him like some odour?

Only later I learnt the meaning of the word
and I didn't hold my breath at all.
I seem to see the old priest in the pinewood,
long since burnt, bending over

miasmal texts which were a balsam for him.
And the odour that comes out has nothing
to do with the divine or the demoniac,
whispers of voices, neumes whose only trace
is found in some illegible papers.

HIGH WATERS

I am on my knees, delirious with love,
at the fountain of Castalia,
but not even a trickle of water
reflected my image.

I've never seen the waters of the piranha.
Whoever plunges into them
returns a fleshless skeleton to the shore.

And yet
other waters work with us,
for us and on us, with an indifferent
and monstrous process of recovery.
The waters take back what they have given:
they are helped by time, their invisible double;
and a flaccid, swollen rinsing
has been robbing us ever since we
left off our flippers to put forth
limbs, a malformation, a joke
which has saddled us with
bad conscience and responsibility.

It seemed that the boiling rubbish facing me
— wreckage, cases, cars
piled up in the courtyard, the smoky
flow which goes its own way
and ignores our existence —
was a final proof that we are here
for something like a pitfall or a goal.
It seemed so once, but not now . . .
At other times chestnuts exploded
in the embers, some wicks glowed
on the Christmas gifts. Now
the demon of the waters doesn't want
to admit that we, his spectators
and accomplices, are still ourselves.

FAME AND THE INTERNAL REVENUE

They telephoned to ask what I think
of Dido and other such goddesses
now resurrected on television;
but the classics are high up, hardly
accessible even with a ladder.
Later on the bookshelf touched the sky,
the clouds, and has disappeared from memory.
Nothing remains of the classics except
bottles brandished like rapiers
by a television charlatan. Nothing
of what's true except the fingerprints
left by a Monsieur Travet

on crumpled sheets loosely held together
by a pin. There's neither Dido
nor any other immortal in there.
Neither sorrow nor joy, only
a cipher and a little dirt.

NOCTURNE

Perhaps Minerva's owl is about
to unfold its wings.
But there is no stoppage of supplies of the stock
for a sale of which we are merely the remainder
to be sold off in a clearance.
And yet we had created with pride
in our own likeness the great robot
of a fluent and greedy infinity.
O blue skies, o noble commerce
and not merely with the Celestials!
Now even the Goddess, our maid and mistress,
closes her eyes so as not to see us.

FIGURES OF SPEECH

Enraptured by his hypallage the poet
heaved a sigh of relief but there was

a gap in the poem which widened,
became a chasm and hurled him into
a cellar where they put traps for tropes.
Nothing remained of him.
Only some Figure, obsolete trash,
said it was better like that.

VERBOTEN

They say that in Kafka's grammar
the future tense is missing.
This is the discovery of one who maintained
the incognito and with good reason.
No doubt he fears the flagrant
or even conflagrant consequences
of his stroke of genius. And Kafka himself,
the sinister croaker, would go
to the stake in effigies or in his works,
which are moreover largely unsold.

KINGFISHER

We carefully practised *carpe diem;*
tried to catch whoever had skin or excrescences,
cast the hook without its being bitten

by tench or barbel (not to mention
trout). Now the situation is reversed
and we are anxiously waiting here for a line
to catch us. But the Fisherman shilly-shallies
because even in a paper bag or
as a carp our pulp no longer
attracts customers.

THE CARILLON PENDULUM CLOCK

The old pendulum clock with the carillon
came from France perhaps
at the time of the Second Empire.
So faint was its voice that it neither
trilled nor pealed but exhaled
instead of sounding, the entrance
of Escamillo or the bells of Corneville
which were its novelty when someone bought it,
perhaps the great-grandfather who ended up
in a lunatic asylum and was buried
without regrets, obituary or other
such notices which might have embarrassed
his unborn grandchildren. They came later
and lived without remembering him
who carried that object within
inhospitable walls lashed by
the furies of the southwest gales
— and which of them heard its alarm?

It was a call that of course woke no one who wasn't
already awake. Only I, being always sleepless,
heard one dawn the vocal ectoplasm,
the echo of the *toriada*, but just for a second.
Then the voice from the case didn't die out
but spoke almost inaudibly and said
there isn't a spring nor electric charge
that won't run down one day.
I who was Time, abandon it,
and say to you, my only listener,
try to live outside of time,
which no one can measure. Then the voice
was silent and the clock remained
hung on the wall for years.
Probably one can still trace its outline
        on the plaster.

THERE ARE THOSE WHO DIE

There are those who die for us.
It happens every day
and it happens to me too for someone.
What a horrible sacrifice this compensation
which should save us all *en bloc*,
fine tourists who spend little and see nothing.

Thus theology, economy, semeiology
and cybernetics go together,

and still other unknown sciences
in the process of incubation,
of which we shall be the nourishment and poison,
fullness and void.

IN AN "ITALIAN" GARDEN

The old tortoise hobbles along, lurching
because one of its hind legs has been cut off.
When the luxuriant lawn becomes animated,
it's the tortoise that limps invisibly
in geometrical patterns of trefoils
and returns to its refuge. For how
many years? Both the gardener and the owner
are uncertain. Half a century or more.
Or perhaps one would have to go back
to General Pelloux . . .
For the tortoise there is no age, all
infringements are contemporaneous.

ON THE BEACH

Now the light becomes more diffuse.
The last beach umbrellas are still
closed. Then someone comes along

dragging his rubber beach bed.
The herb seller comes and lowers
onto the sand her bulk,
a tangle of varicose veins.
She is a crumbled monolith from
the peaks of Lunigiana.
When she speaks to me I am left breathless,
her words are the Truth.
But soon there will be here a chaotic
mass of flesh, gestures, beards.
All the human lemurs will have
crosses and chains round their necks.
So much religion!
And there was someone so deluded as to think
that he could repeat the exploit of Crusoe!

THE NEW ICONOGRAPHERS

They are compiling the iconography of the greatest
writers and soon the least
will follow. We shall see where they lived,
whether in palaces or in *bidonvilles*,
their schools and latrines, whether inside
or attached to the outside by means
of tubes hanging over pigsties,
we shall study the horoscopes of their ancestors,
offspring and descendants, the roads
they frequented, the brothels, if any

still survive the Honourable Merlin,
we shall touch their clothes, bathrobes and clysters
if they used them, and when and how many,
the menus of hotels, the promissory notes,
the lotions, or portions or decoctions,
the duration of their love affairs, ethereal
or carnivorous, or merely epistolary,
we shall read their medical charts,
analyses and whether reading Baffo
or the Bible sent them to sleep.
                              Thus history neglects all sciences
for the hemorrhoids while Olympic flags
flutter over the pennants
and waves of grapeshot form the outline.

IT WASN'T SO EASY

It wasn't so easy to live
in the horse of Troy.
We were so packed in as to seem
like sardines. Then the others stepped out
but I stayed inside, uncertain
as to the rules of combat.

But I know this now. I didn't know it then,
when I held in reserve the best
of my powers for the final and
decisive act, which was

endless, almost the *auto
sacramental* of the vile
in the hide of a quadruped that was never made.

ANNETTA

Forgive me, Annetta, if my memory
barely reaches you where you are
(certainly not among us, the so-called
living). For years your apparitions
had been rare and unexpected and of course
not willed by you. Even the places
(the customs guards' cliff, the mouth of the Bisagno
where you turned into Daphne) had
no meaning without you. All that remains
is the game of charades, enchained
or embedded as the case might be,
in which you were an expert.
They were real spectacles in miniature.
I played the role of Leonardo
(Bistolfi, alas, not the other),
dressed up as a lion to get
the first prize and as for the nard,
I sprayed myself with perfume. But
the profuse and somewhat sweaty
beard I added wasn't enough.
I needed something more, a living statue
sculptured by me. And it was you

who jumped onto a tottering plinth
of dictionaries, miraculously panting,
while I modelled you with I don't know what
device. It was my only success
as a comic domestic. But I know
that all eyes were fixed on you.
You were the prodigy.

Another time we climbed as far
as the tower where often a solitary
blue thrush used to modulate the motif
which Massenet gave to Des Grieux.
Later I killed one that was perched
on the top of a flagpole: my only
crime for which I can never forgive myself.
But I was mad — not for you, but with youth,
with what's the most ridiculous season
in life. Now I ask myself
what place you had in that season.
Certainly a feeling that was
inexpressible then; and later,
not oblivion but a wound that hurt so much
that it almost made me bleed.
But then you were already dead
and I have never known where or how.
Today I think you were a genius
of pure inexistence, a recognition
real because absurd.
Amazement when incarnate is a flash
that blinds you and goes out.
To endure could well be the effect

of a drug on the created, in a medium
of which one never had any proof.

A MILLENARIAN

It doesn't augment (*sic*) production
if one protects the Alma Mater (Alma?).
Tertium non datur; but there
will be a third, the only man who escaped
from the latest epidemics known.
He will walk in a national park
with its unique specimens, prototypes,
the dog, the elephant, the skeletons
of some mammoths and many mummies
of a *homo sapiens, faber, ludens* or worse.

O voracious hypocrites consume
everything, yourselves included,
as is your lot, but praise
be to the pyromaniac who hastens
what you all want but with a slower
rhythm because it's better to be
the penultimate than the last among the living!
(*Applause and many congratulations.*)

THE DECLINE OF VALUES

I read a graduate student's thesis
on the decline of values. Whoever
falls must have been up on high,
as is obvious, but who could have been so foolish?

Life is neither above nor below,
and still less halfway. It knows
neither up nor down, void nor fullness,
before nor after. And nothing
whatsoever about the present.

Tear up your pages, throw them in a sewer,
take no degree in anything,
and you will be able to say that you were
perhaps alive for a moment or an instant.

SORAPIS, 40 YEARS AGO

I've never much liked mountains,
and I detest the Alps. As to the Andes,
the Cordilleras, I've never seen them.
But the Sierra de Guadarrama ravished me
with its gentle ascent and on the peaks,
fallow deer and stags
according to the tourist brochures.
Only the electric air of the Engadine

overcame us, my little insect,
but it wasn't so rich as to tell us
hic manebimus. As for lakes,
only that of Sorapis was the great
discovery. It was the solitude
of the marmots more often heard
than seen and the air of the Celestials;
but what road leads up there? At first
I travelled alone to see
if your eyes could pierce through the clouds
zigzagging among high slabs of ice.
And the road was so long! Comforted
only in the first stage, through
the thickets of conifers, by
the shrill alarm of the jays.
And then I led you by the hand to the summit,
to an empty hut. That was our lake,
a few spans of water, two lives
too young to be old, and too old
to feel themselves young.
It was then that we discovered what age
means; it has nothing to do with time,
it is something which makes us say
we are here, a miracle that
cannot be repeated. By contrast
youth is the vilest of all illusions.

L'ÉLAN VITAL

It was when they awarded an honorary doctorate
to a certain Lamerdière of Freiburg —
whether in Switzerland or Breisgau doesn't matter.
He came up to the rostrum wrapped
in multicoloured robes and vomited out
his Objurgation. I deplore,
he said, the caterpillar and the inevitable
angelic butterfly that comes out
to extinguish itself in the flame
of a Swedish match. I abhor
what is tenuous, silent, evanescent.
There's no other god than the "Rombo,"
not the fish but universal thunder,
uninterrupted, the antiteleological.
Not the whisper which the sophists call
the *élan vital*. If god
is a word and this word a sound,
such a monstrous roar,
which has no beginning and which
will have no end, is the only
thing which is itself and everything else.
Jove dies, your Excellencies, and
the hymn of the Poet does NOT last.
At this point a jumbo jet burst
my eardrums and I was awakened.

TO CONCLUDE

I charge my descendants (if I have
any) on the literary plane
which is rather improbable, to make
a big bonfire of all that concerns
my life, my actions, my non-actions.
I'm no Leopardi, I leave
little behind me to be burnt,
and it's already too much to live
by percentages. I lived at the rate
of five per cent; don't increase
the dose. And yet
it never rains but it pours.

NOTES

N. B. I quote Montale's explanations verbatim, as conveyed in conversation or in his letters to me.—G. S.

SATURA

Satura: For Montale the word "Satura" represents "a miscellany of diverse genres or various types of poetry." It also suggests the satirical character of the poems in this volume. *Xenia* on the other hand means a gift for the guest or a votive offering. In choosing this name Montale also had in mind Goethe's satirical epigrams entitled *Xenien,* written in collaboration with Schiller.

Xenia I

1 *Mosca:* Montale's wife, Drusilla Tanzi, was generally known as Mosca, which in Italian means a fly. Hence the allusion to "antennae" in the second poem.
Deutero-Isaiah: a second or later Isaiah to whom some attribute Isaiah 40–56.

3 *automatic charge:* Montale explicates "la carica meccanica" as the desire which makes the poet look for the girls at the switchboard — a sort of psychological mechanism.

3 *your hotel in Venice:* the Hotel Danieli.

6 *neòteroi:* Greek for "newer"; refers to the "Decadent" poets of the Augustan age, who belonged to the school of Catullus. In the seventeenth century the word was commonly used in relation to those writers who went to the Greek classics for inspiration. Montale uses it to indicate generally those poets who aim at linguistic and thematic innovations.

7 *Azucena:* the gypsy mother who appears in Verdi's opera *Il Trovatore.*

8 *Brissago:* a town in the Swiss canton of Ticino, and the name of a type of black cigar which is made there.

10 *St. Anthony:* the patron saint of Padua.
St. Hermes: Hermes, the patron saint of thieves, merchants, and actors. Cf. Shelley: "And this among Gods shall be your gift, / To be considered as the lord of those / Who swindle, house-break, sheep-steal, and shop-lift" ("Homer's Hymn to Mercury").

12 Originally this poem formed part of *Xenia I*. But in the volume *Satura* it has been replaced by another poem.

Xenia II

2 *Mr. Cap:* an imaginary name for an acquaintance.
Celia: one of Mosca's friends; see the poem "Re-emerging from an Infinity of Time" (*Xenia II*, 11).

3 *Canalazzo:* the Grand Canal.

4 *the jaws of Mongibello:* the furnaces of the god Vulcan.
Mangano: the name of a doctor known to Montale and his wife.

6 *Inferno:* the name of a dry wine from Valtellina in Lombardy. Hence the pun on the word "Inferno."

8 *Paradiso:* name of another wine from Valtellina, which is sweet. Hence, again, the pun on the word "Paradiso."

10 *Avenida da Libertade:* the main street in Lisbon.
Carducci: Giosué Carducci, Italian Poet (1835–1907) and Nobel Prize winner (1906).

14 *The flood:* the 1967 flood in Florence which, among other things, damaged or destroyed some of Montale's own belongings, which he had left in a friend's basement when he moved to Milan in 1947.

Du Bos: Charles Du Bos (1883–1939), French critic and author.

Ezra's beard: a seal based on one of Gaudier-Brzeska's drawings of Ezra Pound. Pound also had it made into a ring.

Alain's Valéry: Commentary on Valéry by Alain, pseudonym of Émile Auguste Chartier (1868–1951), French philosopher and essayist.

Canti Orfici: the most important group of poems by the Futurist poet Dino Campana (1885–1932), published in 1914.

The Death of God

Périgourdine: a restaurant in Paris.

the great Abolished: God. (In Italian, "il sommo Emarginato." "Emarginare" means to put aside.)

In the Smoke

Giuba: a brand of cigarette popular in Italy during the Second World War.

Tapping the Phone

In partibus: "in partibus infidelium": in unbelieving countries; a phrase formerly applied to titular bishops in countries where no Catholic hierarchy had been set up.

In pectore: "within the breast," but not yet divulged.

A Letter

negroni: a strong Italian aperitif; *roderer brut:* a champagne.
Respighi: Ottorino Respighi (1879–1937), Italian composer.
Tetrazzini: a famous soprano at the beginning of this century.
Malpighi: Marcello Malpighi (1628–94), a well-known anatomist of Bologna.
Ramerrez-Martinelli: Martinelli, an Italian tenor, who enjoyed great success in the role of Ramerrez in Puccini's opera *The Girl of the Golden West.*
Tullio Carminati: an actor who played alongside Leonora Duse.
Guardian of the Keys: a reference to the porter at the Hotel Danieli in Venice.
Acqua Alta: high waters at Venice.
radoteur: a driveller or dotard.
liquorice made of meconium: a lozenge in which one of the ingredients was the first feces of a newborn child.
the potpourri of the Guest: a mélange of the musical motifs from Franz Lehár's opera *The Count of Luxembourg.*

The Last Shots

Stanislaus: James Joyce's brother Stanislaus Joyce, who gave lessons in English to Mosca during the Second World War.
hellish fly: in English in the text.

The Ghost

Clizia: an imaginary personage mentioned in Montale's earlier books *Le occasioni* and *La bufera e altro;* the Montalian equivalent of Dante's Beatrice.

NOTHING SERIOUS

The Trimurtic Sybil: refers to the Hegelian dialectics of thesis, antithesis, and synthesis.

LA BELLE DAME SANS MERCI

The cantonal seagulls: the gulls on the Lake of Lucerne in Switzerland.

A MONTH AMONG CHILDREN

The game of goose: a game played with counters on a board divided into compartments in some of which a goose is depicted.

WORDS

Fabriano: a town in the Marche in Italy which manufactures a fine handmade rag paper.

UNKNOWN DIVINITIES

Unknown divinities: Hölderlin's belief in terrestrial divinities living in our midst who can be revealed only to poets has a bearing both on the title and the drift of the poem.
Pythias: priestesses of Apollo at Delphi.

THE ARNO AT ROVEZZANO

Rovezzano: a spot on the banks of the Arno in Tuscany.
"toi qui fais l'endormie": a serenade sung by Mephistopheles in Gounod's opera *Faust*.

103

Men Who Turn Back

Men who turn back: the title echoes, with a significant difference, the concluding lines of Montale's poem "Perhaps One Morning While Walking" (*Ossi di seppia*): "and I'll go away quietly/with my secret among men who don't turn."

Mercury's Temples: the temples of the Roman god of commerce; identified with the Greek god Hermes, messenger of the gods and conductor of the souls of the dead to Hades.

The Seasons

almanacs of Barbanera: the name of a popular almanac published at Foligno since 1713, which provides weather forecasts and a list of various fairs all over Italy.

After A Flight

2 *Jaques-Dalcroze:* Swiss creator and teacher of a system of eurythmics used in education.

Le Focette: one of the districts of Marina di Pietrassanta near Viareggio.

4 *Volapük:* a kind of Esperanto.

Guaranì: the language of a group of tribes in southern Brazil and Paraguay.

Charabia: a bizarre, incorrect, and incomprehensible language.

6 *Sant'Anna:* a village in Versilia where five hundred and sixty people were shot dead by the Nazis in August 1944.

Burlamacca: a canal near Viareggio.

Burlamacchi: an Italian Protestant family which fled Italy and took refuge in Geneva during the Counter Reformation.

Caponsacchi: the priest in Browning's poem *The Ring and the Book.*

7 *tombs of Lucumos:* tombs of the Etruscan princes and priests.

Piranesi: Giambattista Piranesi (1720–78), Italian engraver and architect, and author of *Le Carceri (The Prisons).*

8 *si parva licet:* if it is permissible.

thieves' vinegar: an infusion of rosemary tops, sage leaves, etc., in vinegar, formerly esteemed as an antidote against the plague.

Two Venetian Pieces

I *Florian:* a famous café and restaurant in Venice with tables in Saint Mark's square.

Ranzoni: Daniele Ranzoni (1843–89), Italian painter.

Oltrarno: in Florence the left bank of the river Arno.

Biennial Exhibition: an international exhibition of modern art held in Venice.

II *Adrienne Monnier:* she, like her close friend Sylvia Beach, had a literary bookshop in Paris, "La Maison des Amis des Livres," which attracted men of letters from various countries.

Sylvia Beach: (1887–1962), an American who lived in Paris and in 1919 started the famous bookshop "Shakespeare and Company" which published Joyce's *Ulysses* and became the rendezvous of many famous authors—British, American, and French.

Larbaud: Valéry Larbaud (1881–1957), French writer, critic, and novelist.

dying twice: a few years before his death, Hemingway was involved in an air crash and thought to have died. Newspapers throughout the world reported his death and published obituaries.

DOWN THERE

Flatus vocis: a whisper.

REBECCA

Rebecca: see Genesis 24.
wadi: in the Middle East and North Africa, a rocky watercourse, dry except after a heavy rainfall.

DIARIO DEL '71

To Leone Traverso

Leone Traverso: a translator and a friend of Montale's.
neoterist: one who uses new words or expressions. See note
to *Xenia* I, 6.

Poor Art

Sainte-Adresse: a town in northwest France, north of Le
Havre.
Jongkind: Johann Barthold Jongkind (1819–91), Dutch painter
and engraver. He was a pioneer in the study of fleeting
lights and reflections.

The Negative

Venus guides them: cf. Dante:
> "l'acqua ch'io prendo già mai non si corse:
> Minerva spira e conducemi Apollo
> e nove Muse mi dimostran l'Orse."
> > *Paradiso, II, 7–9.*

> "The water which I take was never coursed before;
> Minerva bloweth, Apollo guideth me,
> and the nine Muses point me to the Bears."

To C.

C.: stands for Clizia; see note to "The Ghost."

IN THE COURTYARD

Oncologist: a specialist in tumours.
Gina: the name of Montale's housekeeper.

THE HIDING PLACES

Sils Maria: a mountain resort southwest of Saint-Moritz, Switzerland.
Gubelin: a Swiss automatic watch.

EL DESDICHADO

El Desdichado: Spanish for "The Wretched One" or "The Unfortunate One," title of a poem by Gérard de Nerval.
Karajan: Herbert von Karajan (born 1908), Austrian conductor.

WHERE CHARITY BEGINS

Malvolio: an imaginary person.

THE FIRE

Via Bigli: the street where Montale lives in Milan.

THE FIRST DAYS OF JULY

moratorium: a legal authorisation for the suspension of payment of debts for a given time; the period thus declared.

In Italian the title is *p.p.c:* "per prendere congedo," to take leave.

Chiliasts: millenarians, those who believe that Christ will reign upon earth for a thousand years, a period of great happiness and prosperity.

DIARIO DEL '72

THE SMELL OF HERESY

Tyrrell: George Tyrrell (1861–1909), a priest who played a prominent part in the Modernist controversy. Himself a Modernist, he was a severe critic of the Jesuits.

Barnabite: a member of a religious order named after the Church of Saint Barnabas in Milan and founded in 1530.

In questa tomba oscura: Beethoven's famous setting of a poem by Carpani.

suspended a divinis: suspended from celebrating the Mass and other acts of the divine service.

neumes: in medieval music, a succession of notes sung to one syllable; a sign giving a rough indication of rise or fall of pitch.

HIGH WATERS

Castalia: a fountain on Mount Parnassus, in Greece, sacred to the Muses.

FAME AND THE INTERNAL REVENUE

Travet: protagonist of the Piedmontese play *Le miserie d'monssù Travet* by Vittorio Bersezio (1828–1900).

FIGURES OF SPEECH

hypallage: a figure of speech in which there is a reversal of natural relations of two elements in a proposition: e.g., "he held his nose to a handkerchief."

obsolete trash: Latin, "scruta obsoleta"; "scruta," "trash."

110

Verboten

Verboten: German; "forbidden" or "prohibited."
The sinister croaker: refers to Franz Kafka, whose name means "jackdaw" in Czech.

Kingfisher

tench: a freshwater fish of the carp family, very tenacious of life.
barbel: another freshwater fish of the carp family with beard-like appendages at its mouth.

The Carillon Pendulum Clock

Escamillo: the bullfighter in *Carmen.*
the bells of Corneville: Les Cloches de Corneville (1877), an opera by the French composer Robert Planquette (1848–1903).
inhospitable walls: an echo from Montale's poem "The Customs Guards' House" *(Le occasioni):* "The southwest gale has lashed/its old walls for years."
toriada: a reference to the poem about bullfighting, *La tauriada* (1929), by the Spanish poet Fernando Villaòn (1881–1930).

In an "Italian" Garden

"Italian" Garden: Montale is referring both to the phrase "giardino all'italiana" (a garden divided into neatly arranged flowerbeds) and to the concept of Italy as the garden of Europe, or as Dante called it " 'l giardin de l'imperio." *(Purgatorio* VI, 105)

General Pelloux: Luigi Pelloux (1839–1924), an Italian Minister of War known for his repressive policy against the left-wing parties.

ON THE BEACH

Lunigiana: a district in northwest Tuscany on the Ligurian border.
The exploit of Crusoe: "organized solitude" (Montale).

THE NEW ICONOGRAPHERS

bidonvilles: French for shanty towns.
Merlin law: the law proposed by Signora Merlin, one-time member of the Italian Senate, which has made brothels illegal in Italy since 1958.
Baffo: Giorgio Baffo (1694–1768), a Venetian poet, author of frankly sensuous poems.
Olympic flags: the last three lines refer to the violence at the 1972 Olympic Games in Munich.

IT WASN'T SO EASY

auto sacramental: a one-act eucharistic play performed on Corpus Christi Day in Spanish towns from the thirteenth to the seventeenth centuries; here a symbolic act of purification.

ANNETTA

Annetta: a name Montale gives to a girl he knew.
The customs guards' cliff: again a reference to Montale's poem "The Customs Guards' House."

Bisagno: the name of a small river near Genoa which is no longer extant.

Leonardo Bistolfi: a nineteenth-century Italian sculptor.

Des Grieux: Histoire du Chevalier des Grieux et de Manon Lescaut, a novel by the Abbé Antoine-François Prévost (1697–1763), on which Massenet based an opera.

A Millenarian

Tertium non datur: "the third is not mentioned."

Sorapis, 40 Years Ago

Sorapis: a lake near Cortina D'Ampezzo in the Dolomites.

the Cordilleras: Spanish word for a chain of mountains such as the Andes in South America.

Sierra de Guadarrama: a mountain range in Spain.

the Engadine: a valley in Switzerland near Saint-Moritz.

my little insect: refers to Montale's wife, Mosca.

hic manebimus: "here we shall remain."

L'Élan Vital

Lamerdière: an imaginary person.

Breisgau: the region around Freiburg in Germany.

the inevitable angelic butterfly: cf. Dante: "noi siamo vermi/ nati a formar l'angelica farfalla,/che vola alla giustizia senza schermi"; "perceive ye not that we are worms,/born to form the angelic butterfly/that flieth to judgment without defence?" (*Purgatorio*, X, 124–26).

Rombo: in Italian "rombo" means both "roar" or "rumble," and a kind of fish which resembles a sole.

To Conclude

Leopardi: the Italian poet Giacomo Leopardi (1798–1837) who left much juvenilia and other unpublished material, part of which has now been published.

SELECT BIBLIOGRAPHY

WORKS

Poetry

Ossi di seppia, 1925.

Le occasioni, 1939 (including *La casa dei doganieri e altri versi*, 1932).

Le bufera e altro, 1956 (including *Finisterre*, 1942).

Accordi e pastelli, 1962

Xenia (both text and English translation by G. Singh, Black Sparrow Press and New Directions, Los Angeles and New York, 1970).

Satura (including *Xenia*), 1971.

Diario del '71 e del '72, 1973.

Selected Poems (edited, with introduction and commentary, by G. Singh, preface by Eugenio Montale, Manchester University Press, Manchester, England, 1975).

Prose

Farfalla di Dinard, 1956 (English translation by G. Singh, Alan Ross Ltd., London, 1970, and Kentucky University Press, Lexington, 1971).

Auto da fé, 1966.

Eugenio Montale—Italo Svevo: Lettere, 1966.

117

Fuori di casa, 1968.

La Poesia non esiste, 1971.

Nel nostro tempo, 1973.

Trentadue variazione, 1973.

CRITICISM ON MONTALE IN ENGLISH

Irma Brandeis, "Eugenio Montale," *Saturday Review of Literature* (LXVI, July 18, 1963).

D. S. Carne-Ross, "A Master," *New York Review of Books* (VII, October 20, 1966).

F. J. Jones, "Montale's Dialectic of Memory," *Italian Studies* (Cambridge, England, 1973).

"Mediterranean Man," *The Times Literary Supplement* (January 28, 1965).

Arsi Pipa, *Montale and Dante* (University of Minnesota Press, Minneapolis, 1968).

Mario Praz, "Eliot and Montale," in *T. S. Eliot, A Symposium* (London, 1948).

G. Singh, "Eugenio Montale," *Italian Studies* (Cambridge, England, 1963).
      Eugenio Montale: A Critical Study of His Poetry, Prose and Criticism (New Haven and London, Yale University Press, 1973).
      The Achievement of Eugenio Montale (inaugural lecture, the Queen's University, Belfast, 1972).

Stephen Spender, "The Poetry of Montale," *New York Review of Books* (June 1, 1972).

ENGLISH TRANSLATIONS OF
MONTALE'S EARLIER POETRY

Edith Farnsworth, *Provisional Conclusions* (Henry Regnery Company, Chicago, 1970).

George Kay, *Selected Poems of Montale* (Edinburgh University Press, Edinburgh, 1964).

Robert Lowell, in *Imitations* (Farrar, Straus & Giroux, and Faber & Faber, New York and London, 1962).

Edwin Morgan, *Poems by Eugenio Montale* (University of Reading, Reading, England, 1959).

Selected Poems by Eugenio Montale (New Directions, New York, 1966).

Mario Praz, "Arsenio," *The Criterion*, (VII, 4, 1928).

G. Singh, *Xenia* (Black Sparrow Press and New Directions, Los Angeles and New York, 1970; the text of the two *Xenia* series as well as of some other poems appeared here for the first time in book form before being included in *Satura* in 1971).
    Translations of some poems from *Ossi di seppia, Le occasioni, La bufera e altro* as well as from *Satura*, in *Agenda*, Yeats/Montale number, (Autumn–Winter, London, 1971–72), and in *Mediterranean Review* (New York, Summer, 1972).

INDEX OF TITLES

INDEX OF TITLES